AWAKEN THE LEARNER

Finding the Source of Effective Education

Darrell Scott & Robert J. Marzano

MARZANO
—Research—

RACHEL'S
Challenge
start a chain reaction

555 North Morton Street
Bloomington, IN 47404
888.849.0851
FAX: 866.801.1447

email: info@marzanoresearch.com
marzanoresearch.com

Printed in the United States of America

Library of Congress Control Number: 2014938441

ISBN: 978-0-9913748-1-6 (paperback)

18 17 16 15   5

FSC
www.fsc.org
MIX
Paper from
responsible sources
FSC® C011935

Text Designer: Rian Anderson

Cover Image Designer: Tristan Mraz
Original Illustrations: Julie Duffens

This book is dedicated to four women who have continued to awaken the learner in me. My wife, Sandy Scott, means more to me than words could express and has taught me more than she could ever possibly know. My oldest daughter, Bethanee McCandless, has demonstrated amazing love and guidance to her two adopted children. My middle daughter, Dana Bollwerk, has also been a great example of patience and love to her children. My youngest daughter, Rachel Joy Scott, continues to provide strength and wisdom, long after her death at age seventeen. I love each of you with all my heart.

This book is also dedicated to my lifetime mentor, Bob Mumford. Without his influence and example, this book would not exist.

—Darrell Scott

Over the years, I've had the great pleasure of observing many teachers virtually, face to face, and on video recordings. I almost always come away from such observations with a deep awareness of how difficult the job of teaching is and how important teachers can be in the lives of their students. I also know this from firsthand experience watching my own four children—and now my five grandchildren—matriculate through the public education system. All teachers who change the lives of their students for the better on a daily basis—I dedicate this book to you.

—Bob Marzano

Acknowledgments

We'd like to thank the staff and employees of Rachel's Challenge and Marzano Research for their help with this book—specifically Rob Unger, Paul Jackson, Jim May, Phil Vincent, Mike Scott, Beth Watson, and Julia Simms. A special thanks to Julie Duffens, who created the original illustrations that appear throughout the book.

Table of Contents

About the Authors

Darrell Scott is the founder of the Rachel's Challenge organization. He has spoken to over five million people in live settings around the world and reached millions more through TV channels such as CNN, and programs such as *The Oprah Winfrey Show*, *Larry King Live*, and *The Today Show*. He has authored or coauthored five books, including *Rachel's Tears*, *Rachel Smiles*, and *Chain Reaction: A Call to Compassionate Revolution*, and meets with politicians and educators regularly concerning issues of school violence.

Robert J. Marzano, PhD, is the co-founder and CEO of Marzano Research in Denver, Colorado. During his forty years in the field of education, he has worked with educators as a speaker and trainer and has authored more than thirty books and 150 articles on topics such as instruction, assessment, writing and implementing standards, cognition, effective leadership, and school intervention. His books include *The Art and Science of Teaching*, *Leaders of Learning*, *On Excellence in Teaching*, *Effective Supervision*, *The Classroom Strategies Series*, *Using Common Core Standards to Enhance Classroom Instruction and Assessment*, *Vocabulary for the Common Core*, *Teacher Evaluation That Makes a Difference*, and *A Handbook*

for High Reliability Schools. His practical translations of the most current research and theory into classroom strategies are known internationally and are widely practiced by both teachers and administrators. He received a bachelor's degree from Iona College in New York, a master's degree from Seattle University, and a doctorate from the University of Washington.

About Rachel's Challenge

Rachel's Challenge is an organization responsible for a series of empowerment programs and strategies that help students and adults prevent bullying and allay feelings of isolation and despair by creating a culture of kindness and compassion. The programs are based on the writings and life of seventeen-year-old Rachel Scott, the first student killed at Columbine High School in 1999. During her life, Rachel reached out to those who were different, picked on by others, or new at her school. Shortly before her death she wrote, "I have this theory that if one person can go out of their way to show compassion, then it will start a chain reaction of the same. People will never know how far a little kindness can go."

Rachel's Challenge was founded by Darrell Scott (Rachel's father) and Sandy Scott (Rachel's stepmother) when they realized how Rachel's writings and drawings resonated with her friends and classmates. Although Rachel was a typical teenager with ups and downs, she believed that she would someday change the world. The Scott family tells her story to inspire others toward kindness, compassion, and forgiveness.

More than twenty million people have been touched by Rachel's story. Each year, at least three million more are added to that number. Rachel's Challenge has received nearly five hundred unsolicited emails from students stating that, after hearing Rachel's story, they reached out for help as they were contemplating suicide. Some even say that Rachel saved their lives.

Rachel's Challenge is a nonprofit, nonpolitical, nonreligious organization based in Littleton, Colorado. By turning the story of a tragic death at Columbine High School into a mission for change, Rachel's Challenge helps to create safer learning environments and make a worldwide impact.

About Marzano Research

Marzano Research is a joint venture between Solution Tree and Dr. Robert J. Marzano. Marzano Research combines Dr. Marzano's forty years of educational research with continuous action research in all major areas of schooling in order to provide effective and accessible instructional strategies, leadership strategies, and classroom assessment strategies that are always at the forefront of best practice. By providing such an all-inclusive research-into-practice resource center, Marzano Research provides teachers and principals with the tools they need to effect profound and immediate improvement in student achievement.

Preface

This book includes excerpts from student emails received by Rachel's Challenge. These students heard Rachel's story through Rachel's Challenge programs and experienced life transformations as a result. In many cases, students contemplating or planning suicide changed their minds after hearing Rachel's story at their school. Slight editing has been done to the excerpts to correct spelling and condense the message without taking away from (or adding to) the content. Names and identifying details have also been changed to protect students' identities.

Additional resources (videos, images, and downloads) are referenced throughout the book using URLs and QR codes. Scan the QR code with a smartphone or mobile device equipped with a QR code scanner application, or type the URL into your Internet browser to access the content.

Visit **rachelschallenge.org/PD** to find out more about trainings for educators through Rachel's Challenge.

Visit **marzanoresearch.com** to find out more about Marzano Research.

It is our desire that this book will help you become a better educator!

INTRODUCTION

An Idea Whose Time Has Come

I am not a teacher, but an awakener.

—Robert Frost

This book is the product of a somewhat serendipitous meeting between two individuals who share a common interest—making the experience of school one that not only awakens in students the desire to be everything they can be but also equips them with the requisite skills to do so. Darrell Scott and Robert "Bob" Marzano believe that while this was the original intent of education in the United States, the K–12 system has not yet lived up to this bright promise. Perhaps most importantly, both Darrell and Bob believe that education in the United States is at a place where this promise is finally within reach. However, Darrell and Bob took very different paths to arrive at this common juncture.

Darrell's journey began on April 20, 1999, when his daughter Rachel Joy Scott was the first student killed in the school shooting at Columbine High School in Littleton, Colorado. Rachel had been known among her classmates and peers as someone who reached out to those who had been rejected by others or who needed a friend. During her life, Rachel wrote extensively in six diaries about the character traits she lived out, such as kindness, compassion, forgiveness, and purpose. Soon after Rachel's death, Darrell was invited to speak to a group of lawmakers in Washington, DC. There, he made the case that preventing tragedies like the one at Columbine required a refocusing of the United States' educational system. Specifically, he pointed out that education must focus on building character in students and teaching them principles like the ones Rachel valued: compassion, kindness, and caring. Following his trip to Washington, DC, Darrell had many opportunities to speak to large groups about Rachel and the tragedy at Columbine. To honor his daughter and continue her legacy, Darrell imparted a message of kindness, compassion, hope, and change. He told Rachel's story and challenged others to follow her example.

Again and again, Darrell found himself telling Rachel's story to groups of students in schools. As Darrell told of Rachel's life and death in the form of an assembly program called Rachel's Challenge, he saw transformational changes occurring in young people. Students contemplating suicide changed their minds and found new purpose in life. Bullies renounced their former ways and reached out to students they once tormented, offering kindness and help. Teachers and administrators reported widespread changes in the climate and culture of schools after students heard Rachel's story.

As Darrell interacted with students, teachers, and administrators in schools, he repeatedly asked himself how a tragedy like Rachel's death could have occurred in an American school. These questions led Darrell to investigate the historical foundations of education in the United States, as well as ways to empower individual teachers to foster kindness, compassion, hope, and change in their classrooms every day.

Bob took a more traditional route for educators. In 1967, he got his first education job teaching high school English. Bob thought he would teach for the rest of his life, but when he earned his master's degree, he found that he loved educational research. This realization prompted him to earn his doctoral degree and eventually move to Denver, Colorado, to take a university professorship. Bob taught at the university level for several years until one night when he attended a back-to-school event at his child's school. As he talked to teachers, Bob realized that most of the work that he was doing at the university level was not filtering down to classrooms. Shocked by the realization that he could spend his whole life doing research that didn't actually help teachers in classrooms, he changed the trajectory of his career. Bob left his university position to join an educational research and development firm and started applying research in ways that classroom teachers found helpful and useful. In 2008, Bob founded his own research laboratory to focus even more intensely on this vision of providing clear, practical, concrete guidance to teachers in classrooms.

Bob's wife, Jana, is a psychotherapist. As Bob and Jana both sought to help people through their respective professions, Bob realized that much of the literature Jana was reading applied to the art of teaching as well; after all, motivation and emotional support are crucial elements of education. In 1988, Bob and Jana collaborated on an article that outlined a model of human motivation and cognition. Over the next two decades, Bob used that model to explain how students learn, why they learn, and what keeps them from learning. The model's usefulness and applicability led Bob to aspire toward a vision of schools where students' thoughts, sources of motivation, and emotions are treated as seriously as their retention and application of information.

By 2013, Darrell and Bob had become aware of each other's work and were mutual admirers. However, they were unaware of the fact that they worked only a few miles apart in Denver. An initial introductory meeting turned into a strong friendship and an even stronger commitment to make formal schooling an environment that awakens the learner. This book is the first concrete manifestation of their shared commitment.

Given the different paths taken by Darrell and Bob, this book is organized into two parts. Part I, written by Darrell, paints a picture of awakening the learner that is grounded in Darrell's understanding of philosophy, history, literature, and the sustained transformations in students, teachers, and schools facilitated by Rachel's Challenge. In part II, Bob provides a research-and-theory base that demonstrates how the current system, which is designed to instruct students, can be augmented so it also awakens them.

The visions depicted in these two parts, although written in different voices with different perspectives and examples, are meant to inspire readers to transform teaching and schooling and to provide a roadmap to that end.

Part I

Reaching the Heart, Head, and Hands

CHAPTER 1

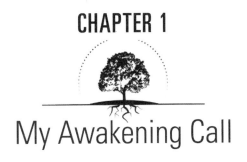

My Awakening Call

*I love you, Rachel, even though I
never met you. Your story inspired me
to share it all around the world.*

—Rebecca

At 11:52 a.m. on April 20, 1999, I received a phone call that forever changed the course of my life. It was a call from my fiancée, Sandy. I will never forget her words: "There has been a shooting at Columbine."

My precious daughter Rachel Joy Scott was the first student killed in the worst high school shooting in U.S. history. Thirteen innocent victims were murdered and others maimed for life. Unfortunately, more school shootings would follow, including the 2012 tragedy at Sandy Hook Elementary School in Newtown, Connecticut.

I have found incredible purpose and meaning in life by sharing my daughter's story and seeing the positive impact it has on the lives of others. I would trade it all to have her back, but I can't do that. Instead, let me share Rachel's story with you.

Rachel's Story

Rachel was the middle child with two older sisters and two younger brothers. She loved life and people. A junior at Columbine

High School when she was killed, Rachel enjoyed drama and performed the lead role in the spring play. She was energized by being around people and could light up a room with her presence (see figure 1.1).

Figure 1.1: Rachel Joy Scott.

Rachel was a normal teenager who experienced struggles and made mistakes like everybody else. However, she found a way to see through her frustrations to a bigger purpose. Rachel had compassion for people less fortunate than she and always tried to reach out to people with social, mental, or physical handicaps. Rachel learned the power of simple compliments and acts of kindness at an early age.

Visit **rachelschallenge.org/Rachel** to find out more about Rachel and to hear her sister Dana talk about her.

Rachel had strong premonitions that her life would not be long but would have an impact on the lives of millions of people. When she was only thirteen, she drew an outline of her hands on the back of her dresser (see figure 1.2) and wrote, "These hands belong to Rachel Joy Scott and will someday touch millions of people's hearts."

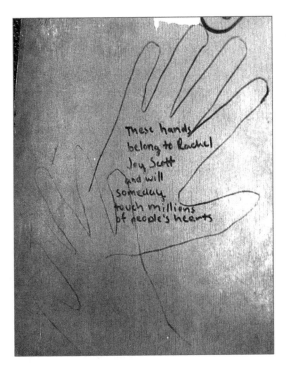

Figure 1.2: Rachel's hands.

Rachel shared her sense of destiny with a number of her friends and family shortly before she died. On several occasions, she told her cousin Jeff Scott that she would not live to be very old. She shared with her friend Nick Baumgart that she was going to die young but that her life was going to have an impact on the planet. She also told her friend Sarah Bay that she would not live long enough to go to college like all her other friends.

Rachel wrote a number of pieces that alluded to her early death. Just eleven months before she was murdered at Columbine, Rachel penned a prayer that referred to her "last year" and a poem in which she referred to her death as "homicide" (see figures 1.3 and 1.4).

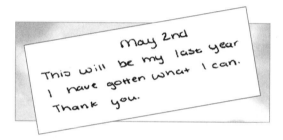

Figure 1.3: Excerpt from Rachel's journal (May 2, 1998).

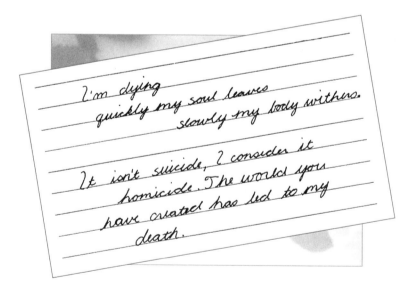

Figure 1.4: Excerpt from Rachel's journal (undated).

She seemed to be at peace with her premonitions, never morbid or fatalistic. Her friend Nick said, "She knew she was going to die young, she knew she was going to impact this planet, and, in the end, that's exactly what she did." Rachel knew her life was going to matter.

After the tragedy at Columbine, thirteen memorial crosses were erected behind Columbine High School. On Rachel's cross, I wrote, "Your life was so full and meaningful and your death will not be in vain" (see figure 1.5).

Figure 1.5: Rachel's memorial cross.

I sincerely hope that you never experience the horror of losing a child. If you have, then you and I share a bond of grief that is indescribable. Parents who have lost a child often feel a need to make sure that their child is not forgotten. For me, amid the grief and emotion of the loss, there seemed to be an overwhelming sense of destiny connected to Rachel's life.

My Story

Looking back, Rachel's death at Columbine was the catalyst for a series of events that has transformed the lives of millions of people in North America and around the world. Those events have been a source of growth and transformation for me, too. Allow me to share my own story with you, starting with a phone call I received about a month after the shootings at Columbine.

The call was from Washington, DC, asking me to speak at a Congressional House Judiciary Committee meeting on the issue of gun control. I agreed to speak, but on the condition that I could speak from my heart—and not about gun control. I am in favor of anything that will prevent violence, but I felt there were deeper issues that needed to be addressed.

Visit **rachelschallenge.org/congress** to hear part of Darrell's speech.

As I explained to the committee on May 27, 1999 (just a month and a week after Rachel was killed), we must put more of our time, effort, and money into helping develop character in the lives of our children. It was not a gun that made the decision to kill my daughter; it was two young men.

Two weeks after speaking in Washington, I received another phone call, which added an unexpected dimension to Rachel's story. It was from an Ohio businessman named Frank Amedia. Frank explained that we had never met but that he had watched the televised broadcast of Rachel's funeral and had been experiencing a recurring dream ever since. Frank felt compelled to share his dream with Rachel's family. He explained, "In my dream, I see Rachel's eyes, and there are tears flowing from her eyes. The tears are watering something growing out of the ground. Life is coming out of the ground from her tears" (personal communication, June 10, 1999). I told Frank that the dream didn't have any particular significance for me, but I wrote down his contact information and promised to call him if it meant something to another member of our family. I thought I would never talk to him again.

A week later, I received a call from the Jefferson County Sheriff's Office. They were ready to release Rachel's backpack and some of her personal items. I rushed over to get them and took them out to my car, where I sat with tears in my eyes. I felt an overwhelming sense of Rachel's presence as I held her bullet-riddled backpack in my lap. I opened it slowly and took out her checkbook, some pencils and a pen, a beret, and some of her schoolbooks. And then, at the bottom of her backpack, I saw her diary. Like any parent who has just lost a child, I wanted to read the last thing Rachel had written before she was killed. I turned to the last page and was absolutely shocked by what I saw.

As shown in figure 1.6 (page 14), Rachel had drawn a rose with dark drops falling from it. Above the rose is a drawing of two eyes. Clear tears fall from the eyes and appear to be watering the rose. I immediately remembered Frank Amedia's dream. I also made other connections between Rachel's drawing and her death. For example, there are thirteen clear teardrops, and there were thirteen people killed at Columbine: twelve students and a teacher.

I later found out from one of Rachel's teachers, Mrs. Carruthers, that Rachel had drawn this picture in class about twenty minutes before she was shot and killed. Mrs. Carruthers said that she asked Rachel what she was drawing and Rachel said, "Oh, Mrs. Carruthers, it's not finished, but I was inspired to draw this. Mrs. Carruthers, I'm going to have an impact on the world!"

Visit **rachelschallenge.org/drawing** to hear Mrs. Carruthers talk about seeing Rachel draw the tears and rose.

Figure 1.6: Picture drawn by Rachel on the day of her death.

This series of events led me and my wife to found Rachel's Challenge, a nonprofit organization that has impacted millions of lives. By 2014, Rachel's Challenge had reached over twenty million people in live settings and hundreds of millions more through television, newspapers, magazines, books, and the Internet. Rachel's Challenge presenters speak to approximately three million students, teachers, and parents every year.

Discovering My *Why*

For thirteen years, Rachel's Challenge has focused on developing and delivering powerful programs for students. As a result of sharing Rachel's story, we have seen schools changed into places where students care about each other, respect their teachers, and engage in meaningful service to their communities.

However, I've felt that there is more that Rachel's Challenge can do. One of our presenters, Peter DeAnello, is an actor, acting coach, and theatrical agent. Peter also helps train other Rachel's Challenge presenters. One of the questions he asks them is, "What's your *why*?" Peter explains that unless a person really understands *why* he or she is motivated to act and think in various circumstances and relationships, he or she won't find satisfaction or fulfillment in life. Without a compelling *why*, people are likely to be frustrated, disengaged, and unfulfilled.

When I first heard Peter explain the concept of *why*, I had been telling Rachel's story for twelve years. Right after her death, my *why* was simply to honor her and tell her remarkable story. What parent wouldn't be motivated to do that? However, over the years, my *why* has matured into a broader purpose. I've had opportunities to talk with thousands of educators at hundreds of schools, and I've seen the impact of Rachel's story on hundreds of thousands of students. These opportunities have prompted me to more closely examine our current educational system, look for ways to encourage change in it, and investigate how education has developed over the past two centuries. Schools didn't used to be sites of violence. Tragedies such as those at Jonesboro, Paducah, Columbine, Virginia Tech, Sandy Hook, and other schools seem to be a relatively recent phenomenon. My goal in this book is to share the results of my investigation and help educators at every level understand how they can change the climate of their classrooms in the same way that we do when we tell Rachel's story.

While Rachel's Challenge will continue on with its original mission, we have launched a campaign called Awaken the Learner. Our goal is to inspire and equip the adults who work with and around students. This book is a plea from a father who lost a daughter in one of the most violent school shootings in our history—a plea for teachers and other adults to consider the principles and philosophies of educators who, not so long ago, expressed ideas and wisdom about how to awaken and develop learners. I believe that these principles and philosophies contain some of the answers to the complex problems of school violence and effective education. Fundamentally, these principles and philosophies are based on helping students *experience* truth, rather than just *hearing* about it.

Experiencing Truth

When I was in the eighth grade, I memorized the Gettysburg Address. It was an agonizing process but a requirement to pass a test in history class. It wasn't until thirty years later that I realized the profound ideas and rich connotations expressed by Lincoln's words. While on a trip to Pennsylvania, I visited Gettysburg. Walking along the trails of the battlefield in the early morning fog, I found an engraved plaque marking the place where Lincoln stood as he delivered his speech. Until I stood on that spot and gazed at the beautiful rolling hills, antique cannons, and stone walls of the historic battlefield, I wasn't fully aware of the magnitude of the battle or the implications of Lincoln's reference to "hallowed ground." What if I could have experienced those things while I was memorizing the speech?

Obviously, my teacher could not take me to Gettysburg while I was learning that speech, but she could have brought Gettysburg to me. Through the use of pictures, music, and stories about the events leading up to the speech, she might have awakened in me the desire to learn more. Better yet, she might have helped me see how Lincoln's experiences led him to write such powerful words and perhaps helped me to recognize the potential for similar words inside myself. Rather than an arduous memorization assignment, the Gettysburg Address could have been an inspirational experience for me.

The goal of the Awaken the Learner campaign is to help teachers influence students on a deeper level—to help them experience truth and find purpose within themselves—rather than just hearing or memorizing information. I believe that when teachers connect with students in meaningful ways, they improve their students' academic achievement, social and emotional skills, and sense of purpose. My goal is to help awaken the learner in you, so that you, in turn, can awaken the learner in your students.

CHAPTER 2

Awaken to Purpose

*Today Rachel's story made me into a
new person. When I walked into the
auditorium I had a bad attitude and
didn't care about anything. When I walked
out I was a different person. I now care
about other people and not just myself.*

—Britney

I am confident that Rachel fulfilled her purpose on this planet.
Millions of people have been touched by her writings, drawings,
and insights from her life. I hope part of Rachel's legacy will be
helping you identify your purpose—your *why*—as an educator.

A Passionate Purpose in Life

Rachel recorded her dreams and frustrations about life in six
diaries. These diaries contain her writing, poetry, and drawings.
On the back of her final diary, she wrote, "When will the world
open and see the art in me?" She answered that question on one of
the last pages of the same diary: "One day the world will see what
I know burns inside of me" (see figure 2.1 on page 20).

Figure 2.1: Rachel's question and answer from her final diary.

Rachel understood the need for a passionate purpose in life. In another diary entry (see figure 2.2), she wrote, "Glory only comes when one pursues their dreams. How many of us know what we really want, and go after it? How many of us have enough trust, strength, and faith to believe that we could do the impossible?"

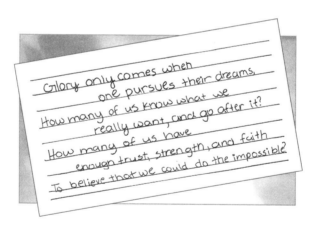

Figure 2.2: Diary entry by Rachel Scott (undated).

Rachel was consumed with a sense of purpose. She wrote about it again in her final diary entry (figure 2.3).

Figure 2.3: Final diary entry by Rachel Scott (undated).

Although Rachel died at age seventeen, her art and her song did not die with her. The world is now seeing what burned inside of her. Rachel's passionate purpose to start a worldwide chain reaction of kindness has become a reality.

After Rachel's death, our family received many invitations to share Rachel's story. We met presidents, celebrities, and other people from many different walks of life.

Visit **rachelschallenge.org/VIP** to see pictures of the Scott family with people who were touched by Rachel's story and to read a letter from President George W. Bush urging people to participate in the acts of kindness encouraged by Rachel's Challenge.

However, the people most touched by Rachel's story have been students. Often, these young people are struggling with finding meaning and purpose in their lives. Every year, we hear from hundreds of students who have climbed out of despair and discovered purpose for their lives as a result of hearing Rachel's story. For example, a seventeen-year-old girl wrote, "The day before you came to my school I was making plans to kill myself. I knew what to do and where to do it. I had just moved away from Florida to get away from my father who repeatedly abused me both mentally and physically. After hearing Rachel's story, I began to dream about going to college and becoming a counselor to help kids get through the same stuff I have been through."

A thirteen-year-old boy said, "I was lost before I saw your program. I was about to lose hope in everything in my life. I used to cut myself, and now I realize how idiotic that was. Thank you for saving my life."

A twelve-year-old boy told us, "I have been abused and treated like crap from day one. I was taken away from my mother when I was five years old. I am currently living in a group home because of my bad behavior. But I just heard your daughter's story, and it inspired me to know that there is help out there. I was going to commit suicide, but this program has inspired me to start a chain reaction of kindness like Rachel did."

A sixteen-year-old girl told us about how Rachel's Challenge impacted her family. "My brother and I just saw Rachel's Challenge at our school yesterday. Our mom came to the evening presentation. I think you saved my family. There was a lot of bad stuff going on at home. People thought we were a perfect family. My brother is a varsity football player and I am a cheerleader, but he was making plans to run away from home and I was planning to commit suicide. Your program changed all of that for us and our mom. Thank you."

These are just a few of the stories that students share with us every time we tell Rachel's story.

Visit **rachelschallenge.org/response** to hear students sharing about their new purpose in life after hearing Rachel's story.

As an educator, you are in a profession that matters. You touch lives in ways that few people can. To some of your students, you will be more of a parent than their biological ones. To others, you will awaken a desire to learn that will stay with them for the rest of their lives. My personal mentor, Bob Mumford, once said, "The only thing worse than failure is succeeding at things that don't matter."

Think ahead to the end of your life. You've celebrated your eightieth birthday, and perhaps don't have much longer to live. As you sit at home one night contemplating your life, you think of childhood friends, people you've worked with, and others you've known over the years. Your memories are a bit faded, like old black-and-white photographs. Some people are difficult to remember; others stand out. Your loved ones are the clearest of all—people you shared your heart with through good times and bad. As you contemplate the end of your life, are you filled with a sense of joy and satisfaction, or are you burdened with disillusionment and regret? John Greenleaf Whittier (1912, p. 152) said, "Of all sad words of tongue or pen, the saddest are these: 'It might have been!'"

For teachers, purpose is not just herding numbers of young people through an educational mill. It is about touching the life of an individual student and awakening the learner on the inside of that young man or woman. It is about leaving a legacy that others will remember as they speak your name many years after you have departed from this life. It is not enough to be in a career that matters; you must find purpose and passion in your profession, or your legacy will be one of frustration instead of fulfillment.

Purpose, Process, and Performance

As I've studied successful educators of the past and present, I've noticed three elements of teaching: purpose, process, and performance. In a healthy classroom, they work in harmony: purpose is *why* students learn, process is *how* they learn, and performance is *what* they can do after learning. In a well-ordered classroom, purpose supports and facilitates process and performance. In the following chapters, I'll explain more about this harmony and how to cultivate it in your own classroom. First, I want to examine each of these elements a bit more closely and look at what happens when one is elevated at the expense of the others.

Purpose

How many of you had a teacher who awakened purpose in you? Mine was Mrs. Cook. She was smart, she cared about me, and more than anything else, I remember her kindness and her consideration of others. She taught us by example that caring for others was more important than anything else.

I'll never forget the Saturday Mrs. Cook came to my house to meet my parents. We were extremely poor. We lived in a one-room shack with one lightbulb in the center of the room and an outhouse about fifty yards away. But the day Mrs. Cook came to visit us, I felt special and valued. She was coming to meet my parents! Later I found out that she went to all of her students' homes and met all of their parents.

One day she asked me to stay after class and said something that awakened the learner in me. She said, "Darrell, you are such a good reader. I think that you are going to be very successful at writing and inspiring other people someday. You are smart and you are a leader. You keep reading and learning as much as you can, because someday you are going to have an impact on this world." Those words of encouragement inspired such confidence in me. They awakened a desire to learn as much as I could, because I knew if Mrs. Cook said it, it had to be true. I was destined to make a difference in this world. And you know what? Those words still motivate me after all these years. Mrs. Cook may have pulled every one of her students aside and told them the same thing, but I sure am glad she did that for me.

Compared to my memories of Mrs. Cook, I remember almost nothing about my other teachers. Mrs. Cook is etched in my memory, not because of what she taught me, but because she awakened purpose in me. That purpose laid a strong foundation for my later learning.

Let me illustrate the foundational importance of purpose with an analogy. My brother was a professional painter for many years. Whenever he painted an outdoor surface, he began with a coat of primer, covered it with a first coat of paint, and then finished with a top coat of paint. Without the primer and first coat of paint, he said, the top coat of paint would quickly crack and peel from being exposed to the elements. The invisible layers helped the visible layer stay in place.

Purpose is like those foundational layers of primer and paint. If we choose to focus on students' passing grades and achievement test scores instead of on their underlying sense of purpose, they may have trouble weathering the storms of life. Just like good painters, great educators want their work to last a lifetime.

Process

My eighth-grade science teacher had a great process for teaching. I don't remember his name, but I do remember that his lessons were well planned and filled with engaging content. Teachers—like my science teacher—who focus on the processes of teaching are often extremely successful. They may win awards, mentor other teachers, lead their department or grade-level team, or train their colleagues on the most effective strategies to use. Emphasizing processes usually leads to well-planned, well-executed lessons. Students often enjoy being in those classes. These are all wonderful benefits, and teachers who focus on processes should be commended for their hard work, dedication, and careful planning.

However, if a teacher focuses on the processes of teaching more than anything else, something will be missing from his or her classroom. My eighth-grade science teacher was a great teacher, but he doesn't stand out in my memory like Mrs. Cook. Why not? I didn't feel like he cared about me. He seemed more interested in the structure of his lessons and the management of his classroom than in the lives of his pupils. I imagine he spent hours planning, but he failed to help us understand *why* learning was important. Merely being a "talking head" is not enough. Raw memorization will not inspire your students. Focusing on the processes of teaching while ignoring the need for passion and purpose can only go so far.

Performance

A story from my childhood illustrates the idea of performance. When I was young, my dad, brother, and I would go fishing in the lakes and rivers near Shreveport, Louisiana. Obviously, fishing is associated with a certain goal: catching fish. However, when we went fishing, it was about something other than that. To this day, the words *going fishing* conjure up the smell of the river, the cypress trees that lined the shore, and the crisp morning air. I remember the time a snake fell from an overhanging tree into the boat and how refreshing it was to dive into the water for a quick swim.

What I don't remember is how many fish we caught. The point of going fishing was spending time with my dad and brother. I also learned to be a good fisherman: how to use a rod and reel, how to change a shear pin in a motor, how to unsnag a line, and how to set the hook on a largemouth bass. With that learning process came more achievement: more fish. But catching fish wasn't the main point of going fishing. Spending time together and learning how to fish were much more important.

Similarly, performances (like grades and test scores) are not the main point of going to school. Focusing on those performances and forgetting about purpose can remove the life from learning. When we are only focused on results, we sabotage the purpose and process of learning and trade a fulfilling life experience for marks on a paper.

Purpose is the *why* of education. Process is the *how* of education. Performance is the *what* (or end result) of education. Without purpose, process and performance are mechanical and devoid of inspiration. To illustrate, consider an American icon: the Harley-Davidson motorcycle. From a performance standpoint, it isn't the best. So why do people buy them? Because Harley-Davidson motorcycles communicate an aura of rugged independence. Owning a Harley says something about the kind of person you are and your purpose in life.

When students' performances don't measure up, we need to go back and examine purpose. Too often, though, we refocus on process. We try to adjust the system instead of the philosophy behind the system. Purpose gives meaning to both the process and the performance.

Purpose-Oriented Teaching

As a teacher, are you focused on purpose, process, or performance? Ask yourself what is most important to you: knowing your students, using great instructional strategies, or students achieving good test scores? All three are important, but the foundation of the last two is the first. Consider the following poem.

"Children of Your Why"
by Darrell Scott

Now performance is important
To accomplish any goal
And the process must be working
For the outcome to unfold.

But the thing that's most important
Isn't what or how or when—
It's the why behind the purpose
That ensures a fruitful end.

For performance without purpose
Is a lifeless piece of art
And process without passion
Is a system without heart.

Let your process and performance
Be the children of your why—
Find your passion and your purpose
And your dreams will ever fly!

As a teacher, you have the opportunity to plant seeds of confidence and vision in the hearts and minds of the students that come through your classroom doors every day. Take the time to pull each of your students aside sometime during the school year and say something that will awaken the learner in him or her.

CHAPTER 3

A Philosophy of Awakening

*Rachel's story has stopped my downward
spiral and saved me from myself. She
has inspired me to thank the people
that I really care about in my life. I
am going to stand up for people who
are being bullied at my school.*

—L. K.

Figure 3.1: Emerson White.

Too often we try to focus on performance by fixating on processes and systems. In addition to adjusting the system, we should also reconsider the philosophy behind the system. In 1901, Emerson White wrote, "All systems of education are based on some philosophic end" (p. 12). White was president of both the National Superintendent's Association and the National Council of Education. He later became president of Purdue University and wrote several teacher training manuals (see figure 3.1).

Visit **rachelschallenge.org/White** to learn more about Emerson White.

As I read White's work and talked to teachers and administrators, I realized that many people are trying to change the current educational system (processes), but fewer are addressing the philosophy underlying that system (purpose).

Philosophies and Systems

A philosophy consists of invisible values, goals, and ideals. The system is the vehicle through which those values, goals, and ideals are expressed. The philosophy is the *why*. The system is the *how*. New philosophies start with passion and purpose and with an organic, flexible approach to bring about positive change. Over time, systems sometimes lose the organic passion of the original philosophy and become rigid, self-preserving organizations with less of the initial motivation to effect positive change.

When I attended school, the philosophy of education seemed focused primarily on educational *processes*: reading, writing, and arithmetic. My perception is that today's philosophy of education focuses primarily on intellectual *performance*: academics, achievement tests, and adequate yearly progress. A dropout rate of over 30 percent (Gonzalez, 2010), low international test scores (Rich, 2012), and high teacher turnover rates (Kain, 2011) all reflect the need for a change in both philosophy and system.

Do you have a personal philosophy of education? Regardless of your school's philosophy or the national educational philosophy, you can choose your own philosophy for your classroom. I encourage you to select one that balances the elements of purpose, process, and performance. The best one I've found so far matches each element to a part of the body: purpose is the *heart*, process is the *head*, and performance is the *hands*.

The Heart, Head, and Hands

The three Hs—heart, head, and hands—were a familiar concept to educators in the 1800s and early 1900s. Chauncey Colegrove (1910), a trainer of teachers at Iowa State Teachers College, wrote:

> We have now pointed out the aims of education in each of its three great divisions, the culture and training of the hand and the body, the head, and the heart. With these broad aims of education all the work of the school should be in harmony. (p. 113)

Charles Oliver Hoyt wrote in 1908 that "harmony between the head, the heart, and the hand [must] be maintained. This gives a threefold division of . . . education" (p. 89). In *The Teacher's Assistant*, Charles Northend (1859) wrote, "True education implies the proper culture of all the faculties of the heart and intellect [head], and the right development of the physical powers [hands]. Of these, the first-named is the most essential" (p. 72). The philosophy of educating the heart, head, and hands (that is, moral, intellectual, and physical growth) was further described by Albert Raub (1883), principal of Teacher's College in Pennsylvania, when he said:

> The chief object of education is development in the fullest sense of the term—intellectual, moral, and physical. That man is best educated whose whole being, body and mind, is most symmetrically and harmoniously developed, and whose powers, both physical and mental, have been strengthened and cultured in accordance with the laws of normal growth. (p. 13)

Gabriel Compayré (1893) wrote:

> There is a physical education, an intellectual education, and a moral education, really distinct from each other, the first tending to develop and strengthen the body; the second, to cultivate the intellectual faculties and impart positive knowledge; the third, to form the heart and the will. (p. 4)

Many people are trying to change the educational system, but very few seem to understand that the system will never change without a shift in philosophy. It is the philosophy that directs the system; the philosophy must be changed before the system can change. Two hundred years ago, a different philosophy drove the U.S. educational system. For example, if you compare the spelling book written by Noah Webster (1857) for third graders with today's third-grade spelling books, you will see a significant difference.

Visit **rachelschallenge.org/Webster** to learn more about Noah Webster.

Webster's speller included vocabulary terms like *mendacity*, *bronchotomy*, and *loquacious*. Today those words might be difficult for many adults to pronounce or define. Words like *kitten*, *house*, and *kitchen* are the norm in many current third-grade spelling programs. This observation prompts the question, "Were third-grade students smarter two hundred years ago?" The answer is no; but the philosophy of education was different then.

As another example, consider the following first-grade mathematics questions:

- How many cubic feet of water does a cistern hold which is 5 ft. square and 3½ ft. deep?

- How many cubic feet of air in a school-room 36 ft. long, 25 ft. wide, and 12 ft. high? If there are 54 persons in the room, how many cubic feet of air to each person?

- How many cubic yards of earth must be removed to excavate a cellar 36 ft. long, 28½ ft. wide, and 6 ft. deep? What will be the cost at 33⅓ cts. a cubic yard? (White, 1890, p. 153)

These are pretty challenging questions for any elementary school student, much less a first grader! I believe that a new philosophy is necessary to awaken learners in the current system: a philosophy of awakening. In the same way that my eighth-grade history teacher could have made the Gettysburg Address come alive for me by telling its story, I want to make the philosophy of the three Hs come alive for you by telling its story.

Johann Pestalozzi

In the mid-1800s, Horace Mann established the first free public school system in America. As a result, most think of him as the father of public education in the United States. But beginning the story with Mann would fail to really explain the origins of the three Hs because there was a "man behind Mann." His name was

Johann Pestalozzi, and my story begins with him (see figure 3.2).

The year was 1798. George Washington was alive, and the ink was still fresh on the U.S. Constitution. But far away in the small village of Stans, Switzerland, people were resisting a different constitution being imposed on them by the French army. Because of their resistance, French troops stormed into town

Figure 3.2: Johann Pestalozzi. and slaughtered over four hundred men, women, and children. In the aftermath of that tragedy, orphans were left in the streets to fend for themselves, sleeping in the open and scrounging through garbage to find food (de Guimps, 1889).

This situation prompted Johann Pestalozzi, a man with a huge heart, to make a choice that would change philosophies and systems of education around the world. He decided to care for the eighty-one orphans that were wandering around Stans with no family, food, or shelter. To achieve this end, he secured the use of an old, dirty, rundown convent to provide shelter and a place to teach the children. Pestalozzi described the atmosphere at the convent:

> Besides basic monetary needs, everything was lacking and the children crowded in the kitchen whilst enough rooms or beds could be prepared for them. . . . I was [sleeping] in a room that was barely the size of 24 square foot. The atmosphere was unhealthy, and the dust-covered walls that lined all corridors made it even more uncomfortable. . . . Many [of the children] came . . . with ingrained scabies, so they could hardly walk, many with badly injured heads, many . . . with eyes full of fear and foreheads full of wrinkles. . . . Out of ten children hardly one knew the alphabet. (as cited in Brühlmeier & Kuhlemann, 2013)

Pestalozzi had no help other than a volunteer house cleaner. He had no curriculum, books, whiteboards, or posters.

Teaching With Objects

With no curriculum or materials to use for teaching, Pestalozzi made use of whatever objects he could find. Flowers, rocks, apples, and any other objects became lessons. For example, holding up an apple, Pestalozzi would ask, "What do you see?" When the children replied that they saw an apple, Pestalozzi would follow up, "What else do you see?" A student might say, "I see a little piece of wood coming out of the top of the apple." This gave Pestalozzi an opportunity to explain why the stem was there and how it connected the apple to the tree branch. To move from teaching botany to teaching philosophy, he might point out that in some way, everything is connected: the apple to the branch, the branch to the tree trunk, the tree trunk to the roots, the roots to the ground, and so on. Because he had no books, everything became his curriculum. While students did chores or played, he found ways to teach them by awakening their interests and curiosities. Field trips to the woods or to neighboring farms also served as lessons (de Guimps, 1889).

Teaching Through Objects

Pestalozzi used whatever was at hand to teach students, and he took advantage of opportunities to extend students' knowledge whenever possible. For example, after students were familiar with an apple, where it came from, and how it showed the interconnectedness of all things, he then asked a deeper question, "What do you see about the apple beyond the use of your physical eyes?" A student might reply, "I see seeds inside the apple." He then asked students to use math skills to answer the question, "How many seeds do you think are in the apple?" One group guessed five, another six, and another eight. Once he cut the apple open, Pestalozzi had them count the seeds. If there were six seeds, he rewarded those who had estimated that number with an apple on which to munch.

Next he asked, "How many apples do you see in this seed?" Students' imaginations went wild! One said, "I see an apple tree growing from that seed that will produce hundreds of apples." Another student (with a more vivid imagination) said, "I see a whole apple orchard growing because of that one seed, and there's a man on a ladder who is picking apples, and he falls and breaks his leg, and his family goes hungry that winter because their dad can't work." Pestalozzi encouraged their creativity, critical thinking, and collaborative communication (de Guimps, 1889).

Teaching About Differences

To broaden the discussion, Pestalozzi showed two different-colored apples to his students and asked them what they saw. He noticed that the children tended to see differences before they recognized similarities. Students replied, "A red apple and a green apple," instead of, "Two apples." He then placed an orange beside the two apples and asked what students saw. This time, they said, "Two apples and an orange," rather than, "A red apple, a green apple, and an orange." The children saw a distinction between the apples until an orange was placed beside them.

Teaching children to appreciate sameness and difference and how to find relatedness and unity were central aspects of Pestalozzi's teaching. For example, he encouraged them to talk about the differences between apples and oranges but then led them into a discussion about their similarities. He pointed out that although they looked different and tasted different, they were both fruits. They were both tasty and edible. Placing a carrot beside the fruits, he again asked his students what they saw. "A carrot and some fruit," they replied. Pestalozzi repeated his request for them to find similarities and differences, this time between fruits and vegetables.

Themes began to emerge from his object lessons and his field trips: unity provides relatedness. Relatedness is expressed through similarities and differences. Pestalozzi held up a rose and asked the children to tell him all the differences they could find on the rose. The children pointed out the petals, the thorns, the stem, the leaves, the roots, and so on. Pestalozzi then pointed out the need for differences on the rose and the need for similarities—the rose needed more than one thorn or one petal. The petals were all similar but different from the thorns. He then talked about how the beauty of the rose came from the relationship between differences and similarities. That relatedness was reflected in the unity of the rose. He talked with them about the fact that all of these differences and similarities emerged from a tiny seed, which was the source of all the unity and relatedness that one can see in a rose.

Differences, Similarities, Relatedness, Unity, and Source

The key to understanding Pestalozzi's philosophy about similarities and differences is this: since we live in a world of matter, we often begin by noticing differences first. A red apple and a green apple are different. When another object (such as an orange) is brought into the picture, we no longer see the distinction between the apples. Rather, we see them as similar to each other and different from the orange. When a carrot is added, we see the distinction between fruits and vegetables. The carrot, as a vegetable, causes us to see similarity between the apples and orange.

The five principles (differences, similarities, relatedness, unity, and source) provide a holistic basis for teaching any subject. For example, in the English language there are differences between the types of words, such as nouns, verbs, adjectives, prepositions, and so on. But as we look closer, there are a number of these words with similarities, such as nouns and pronouns or adverbs and adjectives. We begin to see the relatedness that brings differences and similarities together. The adjectives are related to the nouns. They enhance a noun and give it more character. Connecting nouns and verbs creates sentences. The relatedness of words brings meaning. The relatedness leads to a unity of sentences, paragraphs, and books. If a writer used all verbs, she could never write a book. If she mixed nouns, verbs, and adjectives together without proper relationships to each other, it would appear as gibberish. There must be the right mix of differences, similarities, relatedness, and unity to allow a successful book to be written. The source is the invisible thought behind the words. Without thought, words would not exist.

Math is another subject that begins with differences. The differences between addition, subtraction, multiplication, and division are basic. However, the same numbers are used for different purposes, which highlight their similarities. Relatedness is expressed by questions such as, "If Jim has three apples, and Paul gives him five more, and then he gives one to Sue, how many apples does Jim have left?" This equation involves the relatedness between addition and subtraction. The unity of math is seen by examining how all the operations work together, and the source is the theoretical realm of mathematical thought.

Source produces unity, unity reveals relatedness, and relatedness shows similarities and differences. Source is the origin that expresses outward differences. Great teachers will understand these principles and guide their students from differences to source. To create harmony in the classroom, teachers can help students appreciate their differences and similarities while encouraging relatedness and celebrating unity. The goal is a unified classroom. If our focus is only on differences, we will only see separation and division. If our focus is on relatedness, unity will be the result.

These principles of differences, similarities, relatedness, unity, and source underlie the philosophy of heart, head, and hands. Pestalozzi's philosophy revolutionized education across Europe and in the United States. Horace Mann spent two years in Europe learning as much as he could about Pestalozzi's philosophy and system. He brought that experience back to the United States and created the *Pestalozzian* system of education in the first U.S. public schools. Mann would become known as the father of American public schools, but the man behind Mann was Johann Pestalozzi.

Visit **rachelschallenge.org/Mann** to learn more about Horace Mann.

Friedrich Froebel

As word began to spread about Pestalozzi's success with the orphans in Stans, teachers began to come to Pestalozzi to learn about his revolutionary methods of teaching. One of those teachers was a gentleman from Germany by the name of Friedrich Froebel (see figure 3.3). Froebel left Germany to spend two years in Switzerland with Pestalozzi.

Figure 3.3: Friedrich Froebel.

Froebel returned to Germany with a powerful new philosophy he then refined into an educational system that went far beyond the borders of his homeland. Because the educational system of his day was so structured and stifling, he decided to try to reach children before they entered the system. He created *children's gardens* (in German, *kinder garten*) for very young children. Using music, games, object lessons, field trips, and interactive conversations, Froebel implemented Pestalozzi's philosophy and system of education. He added a deeper philosophical dimension to the things he had learned from Pestalozzi, and in 1826, he authored a book that would become a treasured manual for teachers throughout the next century: *The Education of Man*.

Froebel (1908) stated that learning began with feeling, not with memorization and facts. Students' positive feelings precede lasting impact and change: "We must again awaken in them that inner life of language, of nature-contemplation, and of feeling. . . . Instead of this we put an end to budding life with crude, dead, heartless words, and frighten back into rigid inactivity whatever of life strives to free itself" (pp. 218–219). David Hume (1898), an 18th century philosopher, stated that it is desire (not reason) that governs behavior. When teachers can tap into students' motivations, the *how* will fall into place.

Froebel (1908) also amplified the teaching of Pestalozzi concerning the unfolding of a child's learning process from the inside out. He wrote, "Education should lead and guide man to clearness concerning himself. . . . The inner essence of things is recognized by the innermost spirit (of man) . . . through outward manifestations" (p. 5). Remember Pestalozzi's rose illustration of differences, similarities, relatedness, unity, and source? That principle grew and matured through Froebel's teaching. Froebel (1908) wrote:

> It is the spirit [of unity] alone, then, that makes the school and the school-room; not the increasing analysis and isolation of what is already isolated—a process that has no limits, and supplies ever-new data for further analysis and reduction— but the unification of that which is isolated and separate by attention to the uniting spirit that lives in all isolation and diversity. This it is that makes the school. (p. 134)

Froebel's teachings eventually spread to the United States, where, through the influence of Elizabeth Peabody, they reached a number of the most influential thinkers of the time.

Elizabeth Peabody

The philosophy of the three Hs came to the United States with a woman named Elizabeth Peabody (see figure 3.4). Elizabeth was the sister-in-law of Horace Mann and Nathaniel Hawthorne and had heard much about education from them. Inspired by Pestalozzi and Froebel, Peabody traveled to Germany, where she met Froebel's widow and many of his former students. Armed with Froebel's philosophy and techniques, she returned to the United States and established the first American kindergarten in Boston in 1860.

Figure 3.4: Elizabeth Peabody.

In addition to establishing the first kindergarten, Elizabeth opened several other schools and a retail bookstore. Because of her interest in philosophy, education, and knowledge, she cultivated a circle of friends that included many of the most influential thinkers of her time. At her shop, Peabody's Bookstore, she hosted talks for these friends. An artist's rendering of the attendees of these conversations is shown in figure 3.5.

Figure 3.5: Elizabeth Peabody's circle of friends.

The numbers in figure 3.5 can be used to identify each individual portrayed in the illustration:

1. Elizabeth Peabody
2. Horace Mann

3. Ralph Waldo Emerson
4. Walt Whitman
5. Margaret Fuller
6. Herman Melville
7. Nathaniel Hawthorne
8. Henry Wadsworth Longfellow
9. Julia Ward Howe
10. Henry David Thoreau
11. Amos Bronson Alcott
12. Louisa May Alcott

Wouldn't you love to have been a fly on the wall when those discussions were happening?

I believe there are cycles in almost everything, and there appears to be an effort among leading educators to once again awaken learners by focusing on the heart, head, and hands. For example, the Common Core State Standards focus on communication, collaboration, creativity, and critical thinking. We cannot teach these concepts in a mechanical, lifeless way.

In his last essay in 1967, Bertrand Russell wrote, "There is an artist imprisoned in each one of us. Let him loose." It is your purpose to help find and release the artist in each of your students. You can help students find their song and encourage them to sing it to the world. But first you must release the art and song from within yourself!

CHAPTER 4

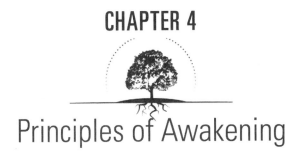

Principles of Awakening

*I had been a mean person, and I was very
sad on the inside. A man came to my school
and talked about Rachel and opened my eyes
to new things. I have decided to help people
who were like me with their problems.*

—Kasey

How can you use the three Hs in your classroom? Start by letting students know you care about them and believe that they can succeed! Give them a purpose for learning. Engage their hearts, and their heads and hands will follow. In this chapter, we'll explore four basic principles that I believe will help you reach students' hearts and inspire purpose in your classroom. These principles are:

1. Reach the heart before the head.
2. Be a candle lighter, not a darkness fighter.
3. Be a see-througher, not a look-atter.
4. Be the change you wish to see.

Reach the Heart Before the Head

Most of us make major decisions from our hearts, not our heads. For example, few of us listen to our heads when looking for a romantic relationship. We see someone we like, feel a pounding in our hearts, and the chase begins! Our hearts are engaged before our minds. When we talk about falling in love, we say "she stole my heart." It is the heart that causes us to engage in relationships, buy products, and undertake projects much more than the head. The following poem highlights this propensity to make decisions (especially relational ones) with our hearts, not our heads.

"How I Chose My Wife" by Darrell Scott

I met a pretty girl today, I analyzed her well
Her stats all seem to be okay, her SATs are swell
Her GPA is very high, her IQ really glows
So if we seem to be a team, then I just might propose!

NOOOO!

My eyes grew bright, my head was light
My stomach started churning
My ears were red—my breathing fled
My neck was really burning

My heart was pounding in my chest
My arms and hands were shakin'
My face was flush, I felt a rush
And both my knees were quakin'

And what I felt just can't be telt
My senses came to life
And I knew she was meant for me
The day I met my wife!

Advertisers learned long ago to appeal to our hearts first before approaching our minds. That's why so many advertisements begin with a baby, a sunset, or an attractive person. Once the heart is engaged, the mind can follow. The first principle that I encourage you to use in your classroom is to reach students' hearts before trying to change what is in their heads.

Be a Candle Lighter, Not a Darkness Fighter

Rachel's Challenge reaches millions of students every year in assemblies and trainings. Our focus is always on being *candle lighters*, rather than *darkness fighters*. Practically, this means we very seldom mention things like bullying when we talk to students. Instead, we talk about kindness and compassion as we tell Rachel's story. Darkness can take many forms: ignorance, bigotry, prejudice, arrogance, or any other thing that robs people of safety and fulfillment. As we've told Rachel's story, we've discovered that the secret to fighting darkness is to be an illuminator. As we shine light, we automatically eliminate darkness. The poem on page 48 expresses this idea.

Visit **rachelschallenge.org/darkness** to see a video of the poem "Darkness Fighter."

Darkness fighters may have good intentions, but they are focusing on the problem. Candle lighters are always focused on the solution: replacing the negative with the positive.

"Darkness Fighter" by Darrell Scott

I cursed the darkness all night long—
It wouldn't go away.
I threatened, yelled, and pleaded
But the dark was here to stay.

I held an anti-darkness sign
But no one there could read it.
It seemed that there was just no way
The dark could be defeated.

I formed the Darkness Fighter Club
To rid us of the plight
And many came, with hearts aflame
To purge the dark of night.

We voted and we passed a bill—
An anti-darkness law—
We shouted at a rally
Till our vocal cords were raw.

We mocked it and we called it names,
We created quite a scandal—
Till someone handed me a match
And helped me light a candle.

Then suddenly the darkness fled—
The room just came alive—
Don't fight the night, just shine a light
And darkness can't survive!

Be a See-Througher, Not a Look-Atter

Bill Sanders, a friend of mine who trains teachers, often encourages them to look past the troublemaker to the kid "having trouble making it." My friend and mentor Norman Grubb (see figure 4.1) told me something once that I never forgot: "If you choose to be a 'see-througher' and not a 'look-atter,' your life will have purpose and meaning."

Figure 4.1: Norman Grubb with Darrell Scott in 1977 and Rachel Scott in 1984.

Norman helped me get through the tragedy at Columbine and the loss of my precious Rachel by helping me see *through* my circumstances instead of looking *at* them. He said, "Darrell, if you can develop a 'single eye' that sees through your circumstances, you will find purpose, even on the worst days of your life." Those words carried me through the darkest time of my existence and took me to a place of purpose that I neither chose nor expected. The following poem is a tribute to this idea that Norman Grubb taught me and all of my children.

"Renew Your View" by Darrell Scott

A wise old man once said to me
"Don't trust the things your eyes can see.
For if you do, you'll know confusion
Always judging by illusion.

Don't look at—see through—my friend,
Beyond the frown, the sneer, the grin—
Peer deep into the living soul
Where beauty, wonders will unfold.

Fear and judgment fall apart
When you're viewing from the heart.
Don't look at—adjust your view
Focus deeper, seeing through."

Rachel also understood the idea of seeing through something instead of looking at it. She wrote about this concept in an essay for one of her classes, titled "My Ethics, My Codes of Life." The following excerpt is from her essay.

Visit **rachelschallenge.org/essay** to read the full text of Rachel's essay, "My Ethics, My Codes of Life."

Excerpt from "My Ethics, My Codes of Life" by Rachel Scott

It wasn't until recently that I learned that the first and the second and the third impressions can be deceitful of what kind of person someone is. For example, imagine you had just met someone, and you speak with them three times in brief everyday conversations. They come off as a harsh, cruel, stubborn, and ignorant person. You reach your judgment based on just these three encounters. Let me ask you something . . . did you ever ask them what their goal in life is, what kind of past they came from, did they experience love, did they experience hurt, did you look into their soul and not just at their appearance?

Notice the last line: "Did you look into their soul and not just at their appearance?" Rachel was a see-througher, not a look-atter! Too often we make snap judgments about people based solely on their appearance or their behavior at a single point in time. It is important, as a teacher, to avoid the trap of first impressions. Instead, seek to look into your students' souls.

William Blake (1917) wrote:

> This life's five windows of the soul
> Distorts the Heavens from pole to pole,
> And leads you to believe a lie
> When you see with, not thro', the eye. (p. 99)

Stephen Covey (2004), author of *The 7 Habits of Highly Effective People*, wrote about how his interpretation of a situation changed when he saw through rather than looking at outward appearances:

> I remember a mini-paradigm shift I experienced one Sunday morning on a subway in New York. People were sitting quietly—some reading newspapers, some lost in thought, some resting with their eyes closed. It was a calm, peaceful scene.
>
> Then suddenly, a man and his children entered the subway car. The children were so loud and rambunctious that instantly the whole climate changed.
>
> The man sat down next to me and closed his eyes, apparently oblivious to the situation. The children were yelling back and forth, throwing things, even grabbing people's papers. It was very disturbing. And yet, the man sitting next to me did nothing.
>
> It was difficult not to feel irritated. I could not believe that he could be so insensitive as to let his children run wild like that and do nothing about it, taking no responsibility at all. It was easy to see that everyone else on the subway felt irritated, too. So finally, with what I felt was unusual patience and restraint, I turned to him and said, "Sir, your children are really disturbing a lot of people. I wonder if you couldn't control them a little more?"
>
> The man lifted his gaze as if to come to a consciousness of the situation for the first time and said softly, "Oh, you're right. I guess I should do something about it. We just came from the hospital where their mother died about an hour ago. I don't know what to think, and I guess they don't know how to handle it either."

Can you imagine what I felt at that moment? My paradigm shifted. Suddenly I *saw* things differently, and because I *saw* differently, I *thought* differently, I *felt* differently, I *behaved* differently. My irritation vanished. I didn't have to worry about controlling my attitude or my behavior; my heart was filled with the man's pain. Feelings of sympathy and compassion flowed freely. "Your wife just died? Oh, I'm so sorry! Can you tell me about it? What can I do to help?" Everything changed in an instant. (pp. 30–31)

One of the young people we heard from after Rachel died was a young girl named Valerie. Val told us that she had been a troublemaker at Columbine, getting into fights and being suspended from school for drug use. She carried a chip on her shoulder, and when people reached out to her, she would react with a "don't bother me" attitude. She told us that Rachel had reached out to her several times. Val responded by ignoring her, but Rachel's kindness was tougher than Valerie's meanness.

Visit **rachelschallenge.org/Val** to watch and listen to Val tell about her interaction with Rachel.

No one understood what Valerie was going through on the inside, and so most people viewed her as someone to be avoided. Valerie said, "Rachel saw right through me. She saw that I was hurting on the inside and really did need a friend who cared about me as a person. She made me want to be a better person." The greatest compliment you can ever receive from a student can be summed up in that statement. Be a see-througher!

Be the Change You Wish to See

Mahatma Gandhi's statement "Be the change you wish to see" (as cited in B'Hahn, 2001, p. 6) remains a challenge to all of us. Students will learn from your teaching, but they will learn even more from your example. They will absorb your knowledge, as well as your attitudes, confidence level, and mannerisms. You cannot escape the fact that you are a model to your students.

One day when my son and I were with Oprah Winfrey on her show, she said, "What we focus on, we become." I have never forgotten that statement. Focus on the problem, and it grows. Focus on the solution, and the problem goes! It depends on where you put your focus. The following poem illustrates this principle through a story.

"Wisdom Replies" by Darrell Scott

A wise man sat on the city wall
When a stranger traveled by—
"What kind of folks live in this town?"
He asked with a heavy sigh.

The wise man answered, "How were folks
In cities where you've been?"
"They're crude and rude, with attitude,"
The stranger said, and then

The wise man slowly cleared his throat
And said, "It's sad, but true—
The people here will be the same
As all those places too."

Another stranger passed his way
And in a little while
He asked the same old question—
But he asked it with a smile.
The wise man answered, "How were folks
In places where you've gone?"
"They're kind and happy," he replied,
"They'll treat you like their own."
The wise man slowly smiled and said,
"My friend, you'll find it's true
That people here will be the same
As all those places too."

We attract to ourselves what we look for in others. Look for the best in those around you and watch your world change for the better! Think about Gandhi (figure 4.2): with only a pair of sandals, a pair of glasses, a robe, a walking stick, and a heart full of purpose for his nation, Gandhi led Indians to free their country from the rule of Great Britain. His integrity and commitment to his purpose on this planet were extraordinary.

Figure 4.2: Mahatma Gandhi.

Ask yourself the question, "Do I have a sense of purpose in life?" If you do, what is it? Defining your *why* and your sense of purpose will help you stick to your calling through the tough challenges of being an educator.

CHAPTER 5

An Atmosphere of Awakening

*It is, in fact, nothing short of a miracle that
the modern methods of instruction have
not yet entirely strangled the holy curiosity
of inquiry; for this delicate little plant,
aside from stimulation, stands mainly in
need of freedom; without this it goes to
wreck and ruin without fail. It is a very
grave mistake to think that the enjoyment
of seeing and searching can be promoted
by means of coercion and a sense of duty.*

—Albert Einstein

How does a teacher combine a commitment to purpose, the three Hs, and the principles from chapter 4 (page 45) to create a classroom where learners are awakened? Figure 5.1 (page 58) expresses my vision of how this can be accomplished.

The tree represents a student whose heart, head, and hands are growing and developing. That tree grew from a tiny seed, which sprouted when it was planted in nutrient-rich soil and a favorable climate. The tree is held in place by its roots: security, identity, and belonging. When all of the foundational pieces—culture, climate, security, identity, belonging, and the proper balance of heart, head, and hands—are in place, the tree produces foliage

Figure 5.1: A visual representation of the Awaken the Learner process.

and fruit: skills, academic achievement, collaboration, critical thinking, communication, creativity, and a positive attitude. In this chapter, I'll examine each element of figure 5.1 and offer practical suggestions to help you awaken the learners in your classroom and school.

Students as Seeds, Not Soil

I used to believe that students were like soil and that teachers planted seeds of knowledge in them. But I've realized that students are not soil; they're seeds. There is a big difference. The first view implies that teachers plant seeds in students' minds and hearts and wait for them to grow. All the teacher has to do is supply the seeds of knowledge: facts, figures, and information. It is up to the student to grow those seeds within the soil of his or her own being. If we view students as soil, they may feel like dirt!

The second view considers students to be seeds instead of soil. Believing that students already have everything built into them for growth and maturity, the teacher provides the right climate and culture for the seeds to flourish. The facts, figures, and information are simply nutrients that the healthy seed can absorb to aid in its growth. Consider this: a watermelon seed does not have to be taught how to produce a watermelon. Everything that seed needs to become a watermelon is already locked inside.

Sometimes a seed can have a very hard outer shell that must be softened before it opens and begins to grow. A teacher who is an awakener will understand this and provide the right climate and culture for the seed to feel safe enough come out of his or her shell. The following poem is based on this view.

"A Seed Succeeds" by Darrell Scott

A flower seed is small indeed—there's nothing much to see
It tumbles down upon the ground beneath a shrub or tree
But deep inside, there does reside a flower unassuming
That in the spring, will do its thing and slowly start a-blooming!
It first must lie beneath the ground, invisible awhile
Until the sun invites it out and greets it with a smile
With culture right and climate bright, that shell will slowly break
And life within will now ascend—a flower will awake
Emerging slow, that plant will grow, and everybody knows
That from that seed, the life indeed will thrill us as a rose!

As a teacher, it is your responsibility to create an environment in which figurative student "seeds" can open, take root, blossom, and bear fruit. That environment consists of two parts, culture and climate.

An Environment That Encourages Growth

As shown in figure 5.2, culture and climate make up the atmosphere that prompts a seed to shed its protective shell and start growing. For success in any learning environment, there must first be an atmosphere of harmony.

Figure 5.2: A visual representation of culture and climate.

Your classroom should be a place where people feel safe. There must be safety before studies, peace before performance, and acceptance before academics. One hundred and sixty thousand students a day skip school because of fear of harassment (Fried & Fried, 1996). Many more go to school with that fear locked up inside of them.

During the 2011 school year, Rachel's Challenge sent out twenty thousand surveys to students who had attended our presentations. The surveys asked questions about school climate and culture before and after students participated in the Rachel's Challenge program. Students returned 9,881 of those surveys, representing close to a 50 percent return rate. One of the questions on the survey was, "Did you feel safe at your school *before* Rachel's Challenge came?" Only 1,464 students—less than 15 percent of respondents—answered yes. However, when asked, "Did you feel safe at your school *after* Rachel's Challenge came?" over 56 percent—or 5,589 students—said they felt safe after participating in the Rachel's Challenge program. Why is that? Can that much change take place in just one day?

What is it about Rachel's Challenge that causes people to come together and feel safe? What is the magic that a total stranger can bring to an auditorium full of disconnected, unruly teens, causing them to hug, cry, and ask forgiveness just one hour later? We believe it has to do with changing the culture of the school and awakening new awareness within each student. Rachel's story is a powerful tool we use to create a culture and climate of safety in the schools we visit. We believe there are tools teachers can use to create the same type of culture and climate in their classrooms. If kids feel safe, they will learn more effectively. The feeling of security makes a huge difference in the ability to learn.

The culture is influenced by the expressions, encouragement, and expectations of the teacher and the students. Climate is affected by factors such as the classroom setup, scenery, and the senses. Here we provide some practical suggestions about how you can address both of these areas.

Culture

There are three elements of culture you can use to cultivate a warm, inviting, safe atmosphere in your classroom:

1. Your expressions
2. Your encouragement
3. Your expectations

Your Expressions

There are two types of expressions you communicate to your students: verbal and nonverbal. Over 70 percent of your impression on students will be communicated nonverbally (Mehrabian, 1972). Ray Birdwhistell, the pioneer of kinesics, estimated that there are around two hundred and fifty thousand human facial expressions (as cited in Pease & Pease, 2004). Fascinatingly, he identified twenty-three distinct eyebrow movements alone.

The first things a student will notice about you are your facial expressions and your body language. To awaken your learners, your expressions and body language must convey warmth and trust. A cold, hard stare can evoke fear or rebellion in a student, while smiling eyes can make you seem more accessible. Do you wrap your arms around yourself, indicating insecurity? The illustration in figure 5.3 shows three individuals displaying various expressions, posture, and gestures. What is each person communicating?

Figure 5.3: Examples of different expressions, postures, and gestures.

In some cases, your words can relay one message while your nonverbal communication states the opposite. It is important to understand the impact of nonverbal communication. Many a student has shut down because of a teacher who was unaware that her facial expression or careless demeanor was hurtful to the student. This is true for all grade levels. If your students believe that you are mean, uncaring, and humorless, they will not open themselves up to your instruction.

There are a number of very insightful books on the subject of expression. We recommend the following as excellent starting points:

- *Nonverbal Communication* (Burgoon, Guerrero, & Floyd, 2009)

- *What Every BODY Is Saying* (Navarro, 2008)

- *Nonverbal Communication: Science and Applications* (Matsumoto, Frank, & Hwang, 2013)

- *Nonverbal Communication in Human Interaction* (Knapp & Hall, 2010)

- *Nonverbal Communication* (Mehrabian, 1972)

Additionally, take some time to look at your expressions in front of a mirror. Examine those expressions that come naturally to you to determine whether they are predominantly positive or negative. Practice positive expressions to become more comfortable with them.

Your Encouragement

Rita Pierson was a great educator who passed away in 2013. Her TED Education Talk, given just before her death, is an invaluable illustration of the power of encouraging students.

 Visit **rachelschallenge.org/Pierson** to see Rita Pierson talk about the power of encouragement in the classroom.

Rita was a master at using positive reinforcement and encouraging words instead of false praise or criticism. There is a big difference between praise and encouragement. Praise should be used sparingly, and only when deserved, while encouragement should be used continually.

Praise can make a person uncomfortable and come across as false flattery. A research study in 1974 showed that too much praise actually lowers a student's confidence in his or her own answers and abilities, as well as reducing the number of verbal responses he or she offers (Rowe, 1974). Here is a list of several things that can provide encouragement to students:

- Stand at the door to greet each student by name as he or she enters.

- Stand by the door to speak an encouraging word as students leave.

- Target one student every day for special encouragement.

- Focus on students' successes, and encourage them if they fail.

Sometimes it is small gestures of encouragement that make big differences.

One particularly powerful way to encourage students is through a project called Classmate of the Week. To implement this project, select a different student to be honored each week of the school year. At the beginning of the year, ask each student to fill out a questionnaire about his or her family, pets, sports, hobbies, likes and dislikes, and so on. When it is a student's week to be honored, post a picture of that student somewhere in the room. Find out his or her favorite song and play it as students come into the room that week. Communicate with the student's parents to let them know their son or daughter will be honored during class and invite them to come and see their child honored. Take a few minutes at the beginning of class to celebrate the Classmate of the Week. Read interesting facts about the student, pass around a greeting card so other students can write notes and encouraging messages to the student being honored, and set up a box on your desk where students can leave encouraging thoughts and comments for the student throughout the week. You may even want to present the student with a small gift to say, "Thank you for being in our class."

Visit **rachelschallenge.org/classmate** for more detailed instructions regarding the Classmate of the Week project.

Your Expectations

Finally, provide high expectations for your students. All students want to succeed (whether they act like it or not), and all students want and need a teacher who believes in them. Don't put limits on what students can and can't do. My daughter Rachel addressed both of those things in a poem she wrote, shown in figure 5.4.

Don't put limits on what I can do
I have faith, why can't you
I wanna show the world what I have
I won't be labled as average

Don't keep me from my dreams
I can reach them if I believe
One day the world will see
What I know burns inside of me

Figure 5.4: A poem by Rachel Scott.

Notice the first line of each paragraph: "Don't put limits on what I can do," and "Don't keep me from my dreams." Don't put limiting expectations on your students.

In 1992, Robert Rosenthal and Lenore Jacobson wrote a book called *Pygmalion in the Classroom*. The book tells the story of experiments in which teachers were told that some of their students had extremely high IQs and were going to "bloom" that year in their class. In fact, all the students in the experiment were normal kids with average IQs. However, students who were labeled as "bloomers" ended up learning more and scoring higher on end-of-year achievement tests than the rest of the students. The high expectations of their teachers made a measureable difference in these students' performance.

Adam Grant (2013) gave another example of this idea. In the 1980s, psychologist Dov Eden studied soldiers in the Israel Defense Forces (IDF). These soldiers are some of the most highly trained in the world. Eden wanted to know if the same effects that Rosenthal and Jacobson found in their experiments could be replicated with soldiers in training. Eden was viewed by the leaders of the IDF as an expert who could spot potential in new trainees. Therefore, he told platoon leaders that certain randomly selected trainees showed more promise than others. Three months later, those trainees that Eden had selected scored higher on expertise tests and weapons evaluations than their peers (Grant, 2013). As with Rosenthal and Jacobson's study, expectations made a difference. As a teacher, you can awaken students and challenge them to levels of learning they did not believe were possible, simply by virtue of your high expectations.

Climate

There are three elements of your classroom's climate that we believe will make it a warm, inviting, and friendly place for students to learn:

1. The setup
2. The scenery
3. The senses

The Setup

The way a classroom is set up has a significant influence on its climate. A 2011 University of Salford study found that a positive classroom environment was associated with as much as a 25 percent gain in student academic achievement. One of the most obvious elements of classroom setup is the seating arrangement. Teachers shared the following observations about seating with me:

- Students tend to sit in the same place every time.

- Rearranging seating can help manage behavior.

- Teachers can help students who are often left out or ignored by seating them around students who tend to be kind and friendly.

- Students who sit in the back of a traditional-style classroom are far less likely to be involved with the lesson and more inclined to chat with peers.

- Rearranging seating can be met with resistance unless students feel that they are involved with the decision.

Many teachers believe that assigned seats are important to ensure classroom control. However, many students feel that assigned seating takes away their freedom of choice and prevents them from sitting with their friends. The following story illustrates how one teacher addressed this tension.

> Miss Johnson stands at the door of her ninth-grade classroom on the first day of school and greets each student with a smile as he or she enters. Her well-decorated classroom is enhanced by music coming from the speakers in the front corners of the room. She has printed "Welcome, my name is Miss Erika Johnson" on the whiteboard. She allows students to sit wherever they desire as they filter into the classroom. After greeting them again, as a group, she says, "I really want this class to be a comfortable place for us to learn and work together this year. Some of you may know each other, and some of you may be new to our school

or town, but throughout the year we will all be getting to know each other better. You are welcome to sit wherever you want during our first week together. You may want to move around and get to know different people, or you may just want to sit with your friends. However, I want us all to be aware of anyone who may feel alone or left out, and include them. And here is something important to remember: with freedom comes responsibility, and if someone misuses his or her freedom by talking out of turn to his or her friend or causing problems for those around him or her, or for me as the teacher, we need to have an understanding on how to handle that situation. I would like to collaborate with you on what we do when a person, for example, may be sitting in the back corner of the room with his or her two friends, continually disrupting the class. I want this to be your decision as well as mine, so if that ever happens, we have all agreed ahead of time on how it will be dealt with. I want you to get into groups of no less than five and no more than seven and come up with three solutions on what we will do when there is a disruptive situation. Your group will then decide which solution seems to be the best. Take five minutes, and then we will discuss each group's solutions to see how many have come up with the same answers. Finally, we will discuss together and decide on the best approach to take."

Of course you, the teacher, will always have the final say on seating arrangements, but by including students in both the seating arrangement and the disciplinary decision, you may have more support and cooperation when changes need to be made.

A number of authors have written books about classroom setup. We have found the following to be particularly helpful:

- *Spaces & Places* (Diller, 2008)

- *Classroom Management That Works* (Marzano, 2003a)

Figure 5.5 depicts various seating arrangements that a teacher might choose.

Traditional Seating: Desks are in rows, all facing the front of the room. This type of setup establishes a climate in which lecturing from the teacher is the norm. However, it can stifle interaction and collaboration between students.

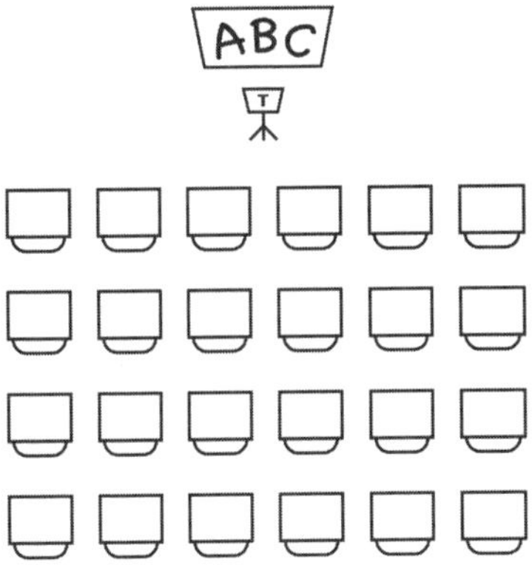

U-Shaped Seating: This setup creates an open, warm atmosphere and provides good visibility for all students. It can be used for lecturing but also encourages discussion among students. Keep in mind, however, that it may not be ideal for collaborative work.

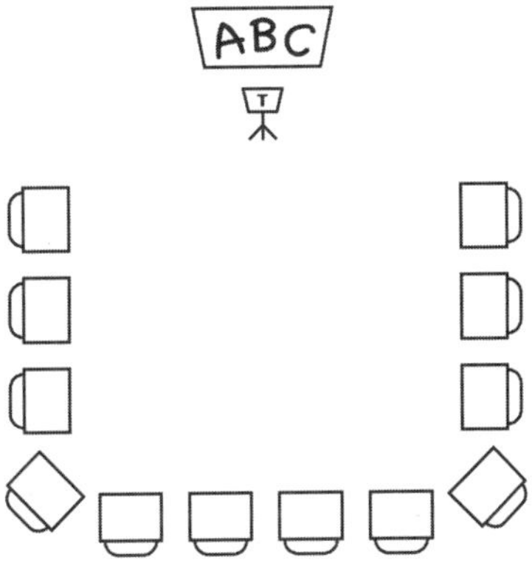

Debate-Style Seating: This arrangement lines desks up in rows facing each other. Teachers might choose to use two rows on either side (as shown) or a single row on each side.

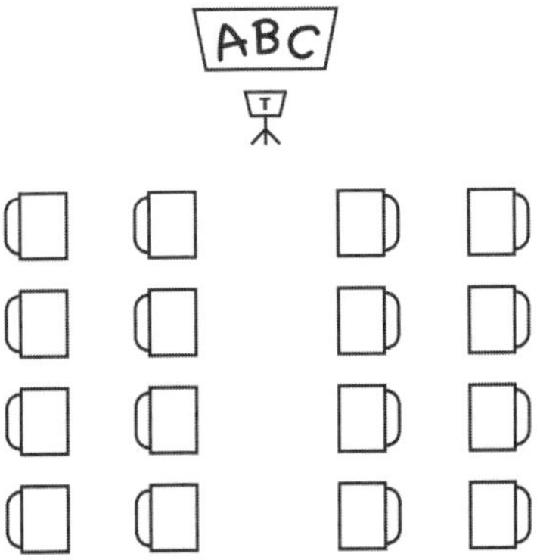

Figure 5.5: Various classroom seating arrangements.

Continued→

Paired Seating: This type of seating works well when resources (such as computers, lab equipment, or print materials) need to be shared. It can also facilitate partner discussions and collaborative work.

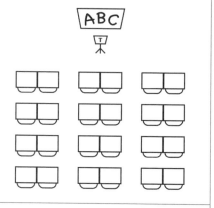

Circular Seating: This arrangement encourages student involvement and discussion by allowing all members of the class to make eye contact with each other. However, it may not work well for group work or lecturing.

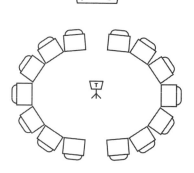

V-Shaped Seating: This arrangement is a bit less casual than U-shaped seating. However, it still results in excellent interaction between students and the teacher.

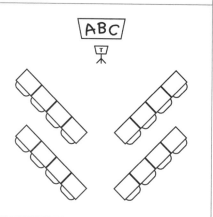

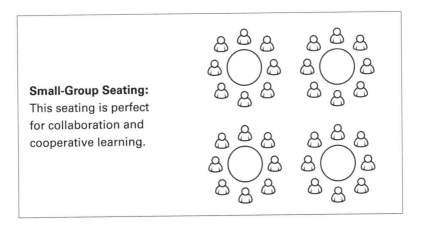

Small-Group Seating:
This seating is perfect for collaboration and cooperative learning.

It is good to keep in mind that seating design may be limited by the shape and size of your classroom. Select the arrangement that best suits your goals and your students' needs.

The Scenery

Scenery involves decorations, pictures, and posters on your walls; "homey" touches (like curtains); and displayed student work. The walls, ceiling, and even the floor of your classroom can be important elements of the climate that students experience. However, be careful not to create clutter and distraction by overdecorating your space.

You may choose to use a seasonal theme or a holiday theme in your classroom. You may also change the scenery of your classroom depending on the subject your students are currently studying. Some teachers select a movie to use as a theme that corresponds with the current topic (such as *Les Misérables* for a unit on social injustice or *Raiders of the Lost Ark* for a unit on archaeology). Famous authors can be good themes for English language arts classrooms, while historic themes (such as ancient Greece or the American Revolution) might be most appropriate for history classrooms. Elementary teachers often use a popular picture-book author (such as Dr. Seuss or Jan Brett) to decorate their classrooms.

Quotes also make excellent décor for classrooms. Quotes might surround a specific topic or be all from one person. One classroom in the Dominican Republic used quotes from Rachel's diaries to decorate. A particularly popular classroom theme at schools where Rachel's Challenge has presented is paper chains. The chains represent the chain reaction of kindness that Rachel started—a chain reaction that students who hear her story are challenged to continue. Each link of the paper chain usually has an act of kindness (that students either performed or witnessed) written on it. In schools and districts where these types of paper chains are used for classroom scenery, school leaders often host Rachel's Rallies at the end of each year. Each classroom brings its paper chains to the rally, and together the school or district celebrates the thousands of acts of kindness that happened throughout the year.

Visit **rachelschallenge.org/chains** to see a video of students bringing their paper chains together during a Rachel's Rally.

The Senses

The final element of classroom climate addressed here is the senses. When students walk into a classroom, all five of their senses begin collecting information about how comfortable, pleasant, or safe that room is. Imagine walking into a classroom partially lit by flickering neon bulbs that reveal old paint peeling off the walls and ceiling. A musty mildew smell invades and offends your nostrils as you walk across worn, faded carpet. The dirty, gray, bare walls display a faded poster that says "Classroom Rules and Regulations." As you glance through streaky, dust-covered windows, you see a nearby street; your ears are assaulted by the beeping of car horns and the irritating sound of continuous traffic. Smelling the pungent diesel fumes from the big trucks rumbling by, you sit down in an uncomfortable chair that rocks back and forth on wobbly legs. You look down at an old desk covered with nicks and scratches. The diesel fumes and mildew are so strong that you can taste them.

This is the worst type of learning environment possible. All five senses—sight, smell, taste, touch, and hearing—have been negatively impacted. In a situation like this, both the teacher and students begin at a huge disadvantage. Fortunately, most classrooms are not as bad as the one described here, but many might benefit from evaluation and improvement.

To evaluate your classroom's sensory appeal, put yourself in your students' shoes. Sit in their chairs to see if they are stable. Listen for intrusive sounds and sniff for offensive odors. Be aware of the lighting, wall colors, cobwebs, and so on.

Unavoidable sounds coming from outside the classroom can be muted or replaced. If your classroom is next to the band room, kitchen, or a noisy street, curtains or wall hangings can help muffle unwanted sounds. Foam mattress toppers make excellent acoustic buffers if you tack them to the walls and cover them with curtains, posters, room dividers, and other more attractive decorations. Cleaning products can eliminate offensive smells. Fresh flowers or air fresheners can help cover bad odors that seem to persist.

Beyond eliminating negative sensory elements, try to positively engage students' senses during lessons. If you are a biology teacher and the lesson involves dissecting a frog, you already have the sense of touch involved. But you can add a creative touch to the lesson by playing a song like Three Dog Night's "Joy to the World" (which begins with the lyrics, "Jeremiah was a bullfrog") as students enter the room. When teaching about agriculture, you might use different spray scents to enhance a discussion about fruits and vegetables. Have your students select appropriate upbeat music that can be played as they enter the classroom. One teacher I know uses slow-paced music with no recognizable lyrics during writing assignments. She uses a particular song to signal students that it is time to wrap up their writing and prepare to move to the next activity.

In this chapter, I introduced the Awaken the Learner model and reviewed the foundational elements that create an atmosphere conducive to student growth and development: climate and culture. In the next chapter, I discuss ways in which students grow and develop, starting with their roots and eventually blossoming and producing fruit.

CHAPTER 6

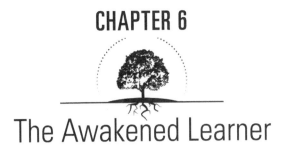

The Awakened Learner

*When you came to my school, I was a
mean person, always bullying others,
but I was very sad inside. I was going
to kill myself—but Rachel's story
opened my eyes to new things. I am
committed now to helping others.*

—K. C.

In the previous chapter, I discussed ways that you can turn
your classroom into a safe, welcoming, growth-conducive
environment that will prompt students to come out of their
shells and begin to grow. When a seed starts to grow, one of
the first things it does is put down roots. Those roots become
the foundation that holds the plant in place. Students also need
roots that will hold them in place during challenging times. Our
Awaken the Learner model focuses on three roots that you, as a
teacher, can help cultivate: security, identity, and belonging (see
figure 6.1 on page 76).

The Los Angeles Police Department (2014) conducted an
investigation into the reasons kids join gangs and identified three
basic needs: security, identity, and belonging. When these needs
are met in healthy, productive ways, students have the freedom

Figure 6.1: A visual representation of security, identity, and belonging.

to focus their energy on learning and growing. In this chapter, I want to explain how these roots affect students' growth and development and what you can do to help them succeed.

Security

Our bodies are made up of many cells that constantly interact with each other. Several major systems work in harmony to provide a healthy, productive life. We have two powerful "security systems" that protect us from danger: the immune system and the adrenal system.

The immune system is designed for security inside our bodies. This system wards off harmful bacteria, fights disease, and automatically triggers healing when we break a bone or cut ourselves. If you have a minor cut on your finger or hand, your immune system immediately sends antibodies and everything else needed to fight the infection, close the wound, and knit the skin back together. You don't even have to think about it—it happens automatically! When our immune system is working, it facilitates clear thinking, digestion, rest, and sleep. All of our blood and energy is centralized when the immune system is operating normally.

The other security system, our adrenal system, is designed to respond to outside threats to the body and often gives people superhuman strength during crises. For example, a 2009 article in *Scientific American* recounted how a man named Tom Boyle lifted a Chevy Camaro off of a young man who was trapped beneath it (Wise, 2009). At that time, the record for a dead lift was 1,008 pounds. A stock Camaro weighs 3,000 pounds. When Boyle later tried to perform the same lift without the benefit of adrenaline, he couldn't budge the car.

The important thing to know about the immune system and the adrenal system is that the immune system is intended to work most of the time. It keeps things in balance and allows growth to take place. The adrenal system is intended only for extreme emergencies, like an encounter with a bear or a snake.

If one hundred sixty thousand students skip school per day because of fear (Fried & Fried, 1996), if one hundred thousand bring guns to school on any given day ("Violence at Schools," n.d.), and if less than 15 percent feel safe at school (Binns & Markow, 1999), what system do you think is working overtime in their bodies? And why is that important for you to know as a teacher? When students' adrenal systems are pumping, their immune systems are not working optimally. Students aren't in any condition to learn when they don't feel safe.

Identity and Belonging

Security is a powerful need, but there are two other needs that are even more powerful: identity and belonging. Students need to know who they are and where they fit in. Kids will do almost anything to fit in. Think about why students form cliques; they want to feel like they are a part of something that gives them meaning and purpose!

Freedom Writers (DeVito, Shamberg, Sher, & LaGravenese, 2007) is a movie (based on a true story) about Erin Gruwell, a first-year teacher who worked at a California high school in the 1990s. Most of her students were gang members, and one of them, a girl named Maria (Eva in the movie), was escorted to class by a police officer. Maria had been given the choice to go to a correctional facility or to school, and she'd chosen school. Erin immediately became aware that her new students had deep needs beyond learning English. This awareness changed her from a transmitter of information to an imparter of hope.

Visit **rachelschallenge.org/Maria** to watch Erin and Maria's encounter on the first day of school.

How do you reach someone like Maria? Erin Gruwell did. She awakened the learner in Maria. Maria now has her master's degree in education, and her goal is to someday be the National Secretary of Education. The first time I met Maria, she pointed at Erin Gruwell and said, "If it wasn't for that woman, I would either be in prison or I would be dead today!" Erin understood that her students needed to feel a sense of belonging in her class.

A New Approach to Diversity

In your classroom, you will likely have many kinds of differences. Students may have differing religious beliefs, ethnic backgrounds, sexual orientations, and socioeconomic statuses. Moreover, they may have a range of attitudes and demeanors. Consider the illustration in figure 6.2.

Figure 6.2: Student attitudes and demeanors.

As you look at the students in figure 6.2, think about them as the notes of a musical scale (do, re, mi, fa, sol, la, and ti). *Do* is standing in the back corner of the room, trying not to be noticed, afraid that someone will find out about the pain and shame she carries from being abused at home. Raging *Re* is taunting and bullying *Fa* and *La*. In the middle of the room, the most popular girl, *Mi*, looks at herself in the mirror while talking incessantly about her summer vacation, her new clothes, and her boyfriend. *Sol* (pronounced so) is slouched down in her seat exuding a "So what?" attitude, and *Ti* is standing by the window, daring anyone to cross his path. The notes of this musical scale are discordant and out of tune. How do you help them work together to create a harmonious melody of learning and discovery? I would like to suggest an approach to diversity that cultivates unity instead of division.

Visit **rachelschallenge.org/mission** to watch a video about the challenges and opportunities teachers face as they bring students into harmony with each other.

Pestalozzi and Froebel (see pages 35–42) saw the beauty of understanding differences, seeing similarities, encouraging relatedness, and celebrating unity. In the illustration of the rose, Pestalozzi helped the children understand that the rose is a union of diverse parts, including the stem, petals, leaves, and thorns. A rose is not all thorns, nor is it all petals. It is the relationship between the stem, petals, leaves, and thorns that produces the beauty of a unified rose. In the same way, when students who are different (in terms of ethnicity, socioeconomic status, sexual orientation, and so on) relate to each other in harmony and goodwill, they understand and appreciate their differences and enjoy their similarities by functioning as a unified group.

If we celebrate diversity without encouraging relatedness, we will never have unity. Diversity and differences must be understood and appreciated as a necessary piece of the overall picture, but if all the petals of a rose created a clique that excluded the leaves and thorns, the rose would not exist. There would only be a pile of rose petals—an incomplete flower.

Educators need to help students see the broader view of unity in which differences and similarities can relate. I've seen clubs that emphasize relatedness and unity throughout the school by including diverse groups, which can have a very positive effect on the school's climate and culture.

The Emphasis of Unity

In *Freedom Writers*, Erin Gruwell emphasized the idea of unity in diversity through a simple game (DeVito et al., 2007). She used a piece of tape to make a line on the floor of her classroom. She explained to students that she'd make a statement, such as "Step to the line if you own the latest Snoop Dogg album," and if the statement applied, students were to step up to the line. Students randomly picked a side of the line to start on, and when they stepped to the line, they were often face to face with peers with whom they thought they had nothing in common. Erin continued, with each question becoming a bit more personal. She said, "Step up to the line if you know someone in jail," and most of the students stepped forward. A few questions later, she dug a little deeper, "Step up to the line if you've lost a friend to gang violence." Again, most of the class stepped forward.

In a classroom so divided by differences—of skin color, of group membership, of experiences—Erin managed to help her students see unity. We use a very similar exercise in our Rachel's Challenge Chain Reaction program, and the same thing happens. When students see both similarities and differences, there is an opportunity for relatedness and unity.

A New Approach to Bullying

As I close this discussion of security, identity, and belonging, let's briefly consider the subject of bullying. As I stated before, when Rachel's Challenge presents in schools, we never mention the word *bully*. We believe there are no bullies, only people who demonstrate bullying behavior. Instead of being *anti*-bullying we are *pro*-kindness, and we believe that the first step in changing bullying behavior is recognizing the difference between the person who is bullying and his or her behavior.

The second step begins with unconditional acceptance of the person who demonstrates bullying behavior. Bullying may be what he or she *does*, but it is not who he or she *is*. Acceptance cannot be faked; you must make a conscious choice to accept and care about the person you want to see changed or change will not occur.

Step three recognizes that ignoring or resisting something often encourages it to grow stronger. Focus on something positive in the person doing the bullying. Don't fight the darkness; turn on the light.

The fourth—and most crucial—step is to reach the heart of the person displaying bullying behavior and help that person *want* to change. You must be willing to encourage and uplift the person while addressing the behavior of bullying. You might say, "Charles, I admire you as a person, but the way I saw you treating Jim is not really who you are." This separates the student from his behavior. Stories can also help reach the hearts of students who exhibit bullying behavior. The stories of kindness and compassion we share through Rachel's Challenge reach the hearts of listeners and create a deep desire in them to become better people.

 Visit **rachelschallenge.org/sorry** to watch the story of one student whose heart was reached by Rachel's story.

You won't be in a position to share Rachel's story with everyone who demonstrates bullying behavior, but you can find ways to touch students' hearts through encouragement, praise for positive behavior, and stories. Sometimes sharing with them the story of the person they have bullied will change their behavior.

Step five's focus is to encourage positive behavior, however slight it may be at first. The sixth step is to model the behavior that you want to see the person copy. The seventh step's focus is to diminish the differences between the person bullying and the person being bullied by helping them see their similarities. Most bullying occurs because of perceived differences. Ethnicity, sexual orientation, socioeconomic status, and physical appearance are often the bases of bullying. When we help people appreciate similarities instead of differences, we can find a place of relatedness that leads to harmony. The following poem highlights this idea.

"We Are Them" by Darrell Scott

Emerging from our common source
We started down this human course
Until illusion blocked our way
And ego taught us what to say

With words like "you" and "them" and
"me"
We lost our true identity
And blinded by our selfish pride
We choked the peace we had inside

So separated from our source
We lived by cunning, wit, and force
Until we came to realize
The emptiness of our disguise

But through humility and grace
We traveled to that quiet place
Of peace and love and harmony
For all of us are one, you see

We ceased from treating others wrong
Our uni-verse became one song
No longer seeing "her" or "him"
'Cause "they" are "us" disguised as
"them"!

Learn to be a peacemaker. The world desperately needs them. When students realize that their differences are not as pronounced as they think, it opens the door for kindness, compassion, and harmony.

Seven Learning Phases

With their roots firmly in place, students can mature and grow upward, using the information and skills they learn in school to produce the foliage and fruit shown in figure 6.3.

Figure 6.3: A visual representation of mature student growth.

There are many different strategies for communicating information and skills to students. Instead of adding more strategies or selecting those I think are best, I'd instead like to simply introduce you to seven phases through which learners move:

1. Imitation
2. Information
3. Conformation
4. Inspiration
5. Transformation
6. Manifestation
7. Impartation

People often experience these phases simultaneously in different areas of life. For example, someone may be in the information stage for one area of learning while being in the transformation stage for another. Here I describe and characterize each of the seven phases.

Imitation

I have had many opportunities to watch and experience the imitation phase. Children often mimic words and actions, even without fully understanding them. For example, one of our sons was working in the garage one day and accidently hit his thumb with a hammer. His reaction was to yell out a word he would never normally say. Within seconds he heard an echo of that same word from his two-year-old daughter, who had just toddled into the garage. For the next three days that word kept popping out of her mouth, often at the most inopportune times! Although imitation is a valid way to teach and learn, it is a very elementary level of education. For most of us it is the first step in learning music, art, language, or any subject. We begin with simple imitation.

Information

As a child develops and grows, he or she eventually moves past the phase of imitation and craves information. Children who endlessly ask "Why?" are in the information stage. Rather than just imitating what they see and hear, they begin to question things and form their own thoughts and opinions about them. They are becoming *informed*. My grandson Brandon nearly drove his entire family insane by incessantly asking "Why?" but his knowledge skyrocketed during that period of his life.

Conformation

As students learn more about the world, they begin to wonder where they fit in. They process the information they have learned and begin to act in ways that conform to what they know about their surroundings. This conformity can be either positive or negative, depending on what students conform to. I've noticed that many middle school students are in the conformation stage of learning. Many of them want to wear the same brand of clothing, the same brand of shoes, and so on. The danger is that these students will choose to conform to standards or ways of behaving that are a waste of their energy. Conforming to the wrong things can make people ineffective because they cannot use their unique abilities to handle situations in new ways.

Inspiration

Conformation comes from outer awareness; inspiration comes from inner awareness. People often move into the inspiration phase because they are moved emotionally by something. It may be a piece of art, a poem, a song, a movie, or a story, but it prompts them to break the boundaries of conformity and explore who they are inside.

Transformation

The prefix *trans-* means *across, beyond,* or *through.* It is seen in words such as *transportation* (which describes a vehicle that takes us beyond where we are) and *transcend* (which means to move beyond the present conditions). If you contrast *conformation* with *transformation*, the only difference is the first part of the words: *con-* (with) and *trans-* (across/beyond/through). However, the results are enormously different. Conformation brings limitation; transformation brings liberation. Transformation takes us beyond ourselves, allowing us to break barriers and do more than we may have originally thought we could.

Manifestation

Ultimately, everything we have learned manifests itself in our lives in one way or another. We can say what we want, but what we truly *believe* will show up in our actions. The transformation that comes from inspiration should result in the manifestation of new behaviors. These actions and choices are sparked from within, rather than by external stimuli. At the level of conformation, we reflect outward influences. At the level of manifestation, we radiate from an inner source. This is the place in life where others want to imitate us, be informed by us, and conform to us. An important choice confronts those at the level of manifestation: will we use what we know to simply inform others, or will we *impart* what we've learned?

Impartation

The final step of educational maturity is impartation. All great teachers go beyond the role of information dispensers. They are able to impart inspiration to their students. They don't just teach math, English, or science. They impart the spirit of those subjects into their students. To use a phrase from chapter 2, they awaken students' purpose. Long after their deaths, their writings, teaching, art, songs, and recorded speeches have the same ability to impart inspiration that brings transformation. I have experienced transformation in my own life through the writings of people like Ralph Waldo Emerson and Henry David Thoreau. I have been lifted to a higher plane through listening to speeches by Winston Churchill, John F. Kennedy, and Martin Luther King Jr. I have been inspired by the art of Rembrandt and Norman Rockwell. The music of Ludwig van Beethoven, The Beatles, and John Barry has prompted me to rise above the mundane to touch the invisible.

Your Personal Journey

The seven levels I've described here apply to teachers and to students. Where are you in your level of learning about being a teacher? If you're a first- or second-year teacher, you might simply be imitating the techniques you've seen other teachers using. You might be collecting information about teaching. If you've been teaching longer, you may have reached the level of conformation. Have you reached inspiration, transformation, and manifestation? Are you an imparter of knowledge to your students or just an informer? You must ascend through the same levels of education that you expect of your students. If you have never been inspired, you cannot inspire them. You cannot teach from a level that you have not reached yourself. However, you can teach students from a higher level while addressing them at a lower level. For example, you can be an imparter who is teaching first-grade students through imitation. I have seen many elementary school teachers inspire and impart while teaching at the imitation and information levels. A great teacher imparts to students every time he or she is around them.

As a teacher, you are on your own personal journey. My hope is that you will engage all seven levels of education. If you do, your students will never forget you. You will impart to them the spirit of the subject you teach, as well as a portion of who you are as a person. Impartation is of the heart, not the head. It is what awakens the learner.

CHAPTER 7

Three Kinds of Truth

My brother and I fought all the time. He is younger than me, and I hated him because every time he cried it was my fault. My parents always gave him more attention than they gave me. I didn't know what to do, so I took it out on other people. I was always depressed and wanted to commit suicide but never could. When I saw the Rachel's Challenge presentation, I couldn't stop crying (but in a good way). I went home and told my parents about it and how I felt about them and my brother, and they understood. My life is so much better now thanks to Rachel's Challenge.

—J. D.

I want to close with one last big idea that has been extremely useful to me throughout my life, and which I hope will be useful to use as you begin to awaken the learners in your classroom. It involves three kinds of truth: methodical, metaphorical, and mystical.

Methodical Truth

Methodical truth is best described as what we can see, feel, taste, touch, hear, and smell. Methodical truth can be verified through our senses and brains. Whenever we analyze, dissect, or define, we are dealing with methodical truth. While methodical truth can be interesting, it can also be lifeless. You can fill students with methodical truth without imparting purpose to them or ever touching their hearts.

Metaphorical Truth

Metaphorical truth is communicated to us through comparisons. When we say "Life is a journey" or "Love is a rose," we mean something beyond what is actually communicated by the words. Where methodical truth is usually communicated through facts, observations, and information, metaphorical truth comes to us through poetry, stories, songs, paintings, and so on. Everyone loves to hear a good story because good stories (real or invented) usually bear some likeness to the reality we know (but find hard to define). Through comparison, we are able to express what might otherwise be inexpressible.

Mystical Truth

Mystical truth is best described as an intuitive sense of truth. By *mystical*, I do not necessarily mean spooky or mysterious. Instead, think about concepts like *joy* or *love* or *suffering*. The words we use to describe those emotions and feelings are a weak attempt to convey the actual experience of them. Actual joy, love, and suffering involve indefinably more than words can express. Mystical truth transcends the physical realm; it can only be experienced. As Bob Mumford used to say, "It's better felt than telt!"

To awaken the learner, you must be prepared to communicate metaphorical and mystical truths to your students. Albert Einstein (1931/2009) said, "Imagination is more important than knowledge" (p. 97) and encouraged parents to read their children fairy tales. Historian and mythologist Heinrich Zimmer said:

> The best things can't be told—they are transcendent, inexpressible truths. The second-best are misunderstood: myths, which are metaphoric attempts to point the way

toward the first. And the third-best have to do with history, science, biography and so on. The only kind of talking that can be understood is this last kind. When you want to talk about the first kind, that which can't be said, you use the third kind as communication to the first. (as cited in Campbell, 2004, p. xxv)

Learning is at its best when both the emotions and intellect are engaged. For example, if you are teaching students about metamorphosis, you can give them methodical truth. Students can read dictionary definitions of *metamorphosis* (for example, "change in form from one stage to the next in the life history of an organism, as from the caterpillar to the pupa and from the pupa to the adult butterfly" [metamorphosis, n.d.]), or they can memorize the steps in metamorphosis, filling out a chart or coloring a picture of a butterfly going through the stages. However, students might learn better if you use metaphorical truth. You could read them a children's book about a caterpillar that goes through all four stages. But best of all, you could help students experience mystical truth by actually bringing butterfly eggs into your classroom and allowing students to watch them transform from caterpillar to pupa to adult butterfly. As they watch their classroom pets change and grow, students will experience truths that could never be otherwise expressed to them. When the heart (emotions), head (intellect), and hands (physical engagement) are all in play, the lesson will become a part of students' identities. Stories are an excellent way to communicate deeper truths to students.

Visit **rachelschallenge.org/butterfly** to watch a video of the poem "Don't Help the Butterfly."

The Power of Stories

Have you ever wondered why certain stories are so powerful? When Rachel's Challenge goes into a school for an assembly, our presenters share a story that reaches students at a metaphorical and mystical level and produces results that go beyond what teachers, parents, and administrators think possible. Rachel's story awakens the desire in people to do what is right toward others. It goes beyond rules and regulations because it comes from an awakened heart. It is organic, not legislated ethics.

Teaching by metaphor is certainly not new. In fact, it may be one of the oldest teaching methods. Think of *Aesop's Fables*. Have you ever wondered why this collection of stories has remained so popular and well known centuries after it was written? It is because the stories communicate with listeners at all three levels of truth. For example, consider the fable of the bundle of sticks:

> There was once a man who had three sons that he loved dearly. However, the boys were always arguing and fighting with each other. He reprimanded them time and time again, but they ignored his rebukes and continued to have their fights. Then one day, he called for them to come, and he handed the oldest a bundle of sticks. He ordered his son to break the bundle, and although the son tried his best, he could not break it. The bundle was then passed on to the other two sons, with the same results. "Now," he said, "I want you to each take one stick from the bundle and see if you can break it." And of course, each son was easily able to break the stick in half. Their father smiled at them and said, "Remember that when you are divided you are weak. When you are united you are strong." The moral of the story: In unity, there is strength. (paraphrased from Jacobs, 1914)

Look carefully at the different elements of this story. The entire tale conveys the mystical idea of unity. That concept is conveyed through a metaphor: unity is a bundle of sticks. Aesop finishes with a methodical truth, which we usually refer to as the *moral*. *Aesop's Fables* are laced with all three kinds of truth and are amazing vehicles to communicate those three kinds of truth to your students. For this reason, part of the Awaken the Learner series of teaching materials includes a series of books called *Timeless Tales to Live By* (Scott, 2013). These books feature modernized versions of *Aesop's Fables*, beautifully illustrated for you to use with you students. Each one is short and includes questions that will help you awaken your students to the truths in each one.

Visit **rachelschallenge.org/timelesstales** to learn more about *Timeless Tales to Live By*.

The Influence of a Story

Take out a dollar bill, and look at the right portion of the back. You should see the great seal of the United States (see figure 7.1).

Figure 7.1: Great seal of the United States (front).

The seal contains a reference to a story very similar to the bundle of sticks tale. Aesop was not the only one to write stories that expressed mystical truths. In fact, the same mystical truth expressed by the fable of the bundle of sticks was expressed by a symbol from a different culture, the Iroquois nation. The Iroquois symbol influenced colonial American leaders to create a union of colonies and separate from England's rule and is now reflected in the great seal of the United States. The Iroquois tale is called "The Bundle of Arrows."

The Iroquois Confederacy (made up of the Cayuga, Mohawk, Oneida, Onondaga, Seneca, and Tuscarora nations) functioned as a democracy long before colonists came from Europe to America. The confederacy was governed by a constitution, which the Iroquois called the Great Law of Peace. Oral tradition within the Great Law used the idea of a bundle of five arrows to illustrate the concept of strength in unity. One arrow by itself is easy to break. Five arrows bundled together are almost impossible to break. Do you recognize any mystical or metaphorical truth?

As Benjamin Franklin and other colonial leaders pondered the possibility of breaking free from England's rule, they looked to the Iroquois Confederacy for guidance. The truth of the Iroquois symbol is reflected in Benjamin Franklin's statement to John Hancock at the signing of the Declaration of Independence. Hancock (who had just signed the Declaration) said, "We must all hang together," to which Franklin replied, "Yes . . . we must, indeed, all hang together, or most assuredly we shall all hang separately" (as cited in Sparks, 1844, p. 408). The mystical truth expressed in Aesop's fable and the Iroquois's symbol is captured in the bundle of arrows clutched together in the eagle's talon on the front of the great seal of the United States. Those thirteen arrows represent the strength of the thirteen colonies bound together in unbreakable unity. In the same way that an Iroquois tale inspired colonial leaders, you too can use stories to inspire your students. I suggest *Aesop's Fables* as an excellent starting point but also recommend including tales and fables from other cultures as well.

The Influence of a Teacher

As I mentioned in chapter 4, Rachel wrote an essay for one of her classes in school shortly before her death, entitled "My Ethics, My Codes of Life." Rachel wasn't just parroting back to her teacher the principles and information that she'd heard from others or been told were right. Instead, she was expressing her personal codes of life. As I close, I want to include another excerpt from Rachel's essay that I hope will inspire you to awaken the learners in your classroom:

> Compassion is the greatest form of love humans have to offer. According to Webster's Dictionary compassion means a feeling of sympathy for another's misfortune. My definition of compassion is forgiving, loving, helping, leading, and showing mercy for others. I have this theory that if one person can go out of their way to show compassion, then it will start a chain reaction of the same. People will never know how far a little kindness can go. [personal essay, undated]

Look back at what Rachel wrote. She touches the methodical when she quotes Webster's Dictionary. She touches the metaphorical when she describes her own definition of compassion. And she reaches into the mystical when she expresses the idea of a chain reaction of kindness that starts with one person and stretches to infinity.

As a teacher, you may feel overwhelmed. You may think you don't have time to awaken your learners. You may feel crushed by the weight of just trying to communicate the information and skills you're expected to teach. You may desperately want to awaken your learners but not know where to start. My hope is that I've given you lots of options throughout the preceding chapters. If those seem like too much to do at once, please listen to the mystical truth that Rachel communicated in her essay. Begin with kindness. Go out of your way to show compassion to your students, and watch them come alive. Reach out to their hearts, and their heads and hands will follow. Awaken them to purpose, and watch them soar. After all, you never know how far a little kindness can go.

Part II

Instructing and Awakening the Learner

CHAPTER 8

Instruct *and* Awaken

The teacher who is indeed wise
does not bid you to enter the house
of his wisdom but rather leads you
to the threshold of your mind.

—Khalil Gibran

In chapters 1–7, Darrell has provided a case for an approach to schooling that awakens the learner. It is a compelling case, as articulated by Darrell, with equal measures of heart and mind. Whether one looks at the historical evidence provided by Friedrich Froebel, Johann Pestalozzi, and Elizabeth Peabody, the current evidence provided by educators like Erin Gruwell, or the continuing evidence of fundamental changes in students, teachers, and administrators generated by Rachel's Challenge, the conclusion is inevitable—schools have the potential and power to awaken the learner. In this chapter and those following, I will place the message of Darrell's preceding chapters in the context of current research and theory in psychology, teaching, and schooling. Virtually all of Darrell's recommendations are supported by that research and theory.

From an educational perspective, Darrell's recommendations might be thought of as a call for an "evocative approach" to K–12 education. The word *evoke* is commonly defined or described as the action of eliciting, stirring up, arousing, calling forth, and so on. To awaken the learner is to evoke something from the learner that he or she already has but is currently dormant, or at least latent. The term *instruct* is commonly described as the action of training, directing, guiding, teaching, and so on. To instruct the learner is to provide something he or she does not yet possess, at least not in full measure.

Instructing the learner and awakening the learner are different ways of looking at and designing education. An approach focused on instructing the learner puts the teacher at the center of the educational process. An approach focused on awakening the learner puts the student at the center. While this dichotomy implies that a choice must be made, there is room—and indeed, a need—for both approaches. However, as Darrell pointed out, the emphasis in U.S. education has historically been on instructing the learner. Therefore adjustments must be made, but wholesale abandonment of the current system is not necessary or advisable. Awakening the learner can fit within the current system, but that system must be adjusted to embrace it fully.

To understand the research and theory underpinning the distinction between instructing the learner and awakening the learner, consider how human beings think and react on a moment-by-moment basis. This model of human behavior has been developed over a number of years (see Marzano, 1998; Marzano & Kendall, 2007; and Marzano & Marzano, 1988, 2010).

How Humans Think and React

At any moment in time, an individual is engaged in or thinking about something. For example, consider a middle school science class in which the teacher is presenting students with information about tides (how they occur, different types, and their effect on human life). One student is looking at the teacher but is actually daydreaming about playing in an upcoming volleyball game. At the moment, she is engaged in or thinking about the volleyball game. The student sitting next to her is not only looking at the teacher but also paying attention to the information about tides. At that moment, the student is engaged in or thinking about tides.

After the presentation, the teacher changes the focus of the class to a questionnaire students need to fill out regarding their opinions about how the school is being run and what can be done to improve it. Both students described previously have to decide whether they will engage in the new task. Figure 8.1 depicts the process involved in making that decision.

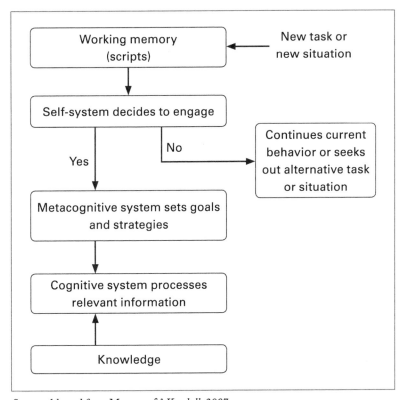

Source: *Adapted from Marzano & Kendall, 2007.*
Figure 8.1: Model of behavior.

The model in figure 8.1 has a number of parts. Consider each of these parts briefly.

New Tasks

At the top right of figure 8.1 is the phrase "New task or new situation." This represents the fact that humans change what they are currently doing when a new task or situation presents itself. This is the case for both students in the science class, because the teacher presented them with the new task of filling out the questionnaire. They can decide whether or not to engage in the new task. If not, they could continue what they are currently doing or seek out an alternative task or situation. The student who is daydreaming could easily continue daydreaming. The student who is paying attention would have to seek out a new activity if she chooses not to fill out the questionnaire, since her current task of paying attention to the teacher has ended of its own accord.

Working Memory

At the top left of the model in figure 8.1 is a box titled "Working memory (scripts)." As its name implies, working memory is where data on which we are currently focused is processed. Stated differently, whatever we are engaged in at any moment is being processed in working memory. The student paying attention to the information about tides is currently processing that information in working memory. The student daydreaming about volleyball is currently processing that information in working memory. For all practical purposes, whatever is in working memory is our experience of life at that moment. No matter what else is occurring, human beings are focused on only one thing moment by moment. Most commonly, working memory is occupied by a script.

The concept of scripts is probably one of the more powerful psychological constructs used to explain human behavior. Oddly enough, the concept of scripts was developed in the field of artificial intelligence (see Schank & Abelson, 1977). Simply stated, a script is a mental structure that describes an appropriate sequence of events in a particular situation. Human beings have scripts for virtually everything they do on a routine basis, like putting on clothes, walking across a busy street, parking a car, and so on.

Students will have scripts for almost everything they do in school, such as talking to friends, meeting new people, talking to a particular teacher, asking for permission to leave the room, and so on. The student paying attention to the presentation about tides is probably following a script, which includes things like:

- Listen to the teacher.

- Occasionally stop and take notes.

- Ask a question if you get confused.

- Raise your hand whenever the teacher asks a question.

Even the student who is focused on the volleyball game is following a script about how to daydream in class without getting into trouble. It might include elements like looking in the teacher's direction while she is presenting, occasionally pretending to take notes, interrupting the daydream every few minutes to determine what's happening in class, and so on.

As mentioned previously, the two students will continue to execute their current scripts until they are presented with a new task or situation. However, to switch attention to a new task or situation, the students will have to elect to do so. The process of making such a decision is controlled by the self-system.

The Self-System

Our self-systems contain our beliefs about life, goals, and desires and make decisions about what we do and don't do. As Barbara McCombs and Robert Marzano (1990) noted:

> The self as agent, as the basis of will and volition, can be thought of, in part, as a generative structure that is goal directed. . . . [It] consciously or unconsciously define[s] who we are, what we think, and what we do. (p. 66)

Our self-system interprets all new tasks and situations that present themselves to us. Based on our interpretations, we either engage in the new task or situation, continue what we are currently doing, or seek alternatives. How the two students interpret the invitation to complete the questionnaire will determine what they do next.

The Metacognitive System

If a new task is selected—that is, if the interpretation rendered by the self-system so dictates—the metacognitive system is engaged. One of the initial jobs of the metacognitive system is to set one or more goals relative to the new task. For example, assume that one of the two students elects to complete the questionnaire. He or she might set a goal to get it done quickly, but to do so in a way that reflects positively on the teacher. Once a goal is set, the student uses processes from the cognitive system.

The Cognitive System

The cognitive system is responsible for analyzing the demands of the new task or situation, making inferences, and drawing conclusions about what should be done. For example, before starting the questionnaire, the student might briefly scan it to get a sense of how long it is, review a few items to see the general tenor of what is being asked, and form conclusions about what the questionnaire is intended to do. The cognitive system uses knowledge.

Knowledge

The component at the bottom of figure 8.1 (page 101) is knowledge. Knowledge is quite important to successfully engaging in a new task or situation. All tasks and situations, even the most mundane, require a certain amount of knowledge. For example, going to the grocery store requires an understanding of how to determine what is in the aisles, how to pay at the register, and so on. Research has found that knowledge has a significant impact on a person's success. Thomas Sticht, C. Richard Hofstetter, and Carolyn Hofstetter (1997) interviewed 538 randomly selected adults and found a significant relationship between individuals' knowledge levels and their "achievement of a higher status occupation and/or . . . an average or higher level of income" (p. 3). In the classroom, a student might be very motivated to engage in a task (self-system), set goals relative to the task (metacognitive system), and have an excellent set of thinking and reasoning skills to apply to the task (cognitive system). However, without the requisite knowledge to successfully engage in the task, the effects of the other systems will be minimal. To return to the previous example, the student engaged in the questionnaire must have an awareness of how to interpret various questions, how to record responses, how to turn in the questionnaire, and so on.

Cultivating Self-Efficacy

The processes of the self-system, metacognitive system, cognitive system, and knowledge describe human functioning well. They also provide a basis for differentiating an education system focused on instructing the learner from one focused on awakening the learner.

Education has historically focused on conveying knowledge and has only recently emphasized the cognitive system by providing students with opportunities to analyze information deeply and rigorously. These are the purview of instructing the learner: conveying new knowledge and deepening that knowledge through rigorous analysis using cognitive skills.

Understanding and using the skills of the self-system and the metacognitive system are at the core of *self-efficacy*, an individual's ability to control his or her own life. This involves self-system components like managing one's interpretations and understanding one's deepest desires. It also involves metacognitive processes like setting personal goals and monitoring progress toward those goals. This is the purview of awakening the learner.

If students are to be prepared for the challenges of the new century, then the education system designed to prepare students must provide them with an awareness and control of all the elements previously described. This is accomplished by creating a system designed to both instruct and awaken the learner. The following chapters describe how this can be done.

CHAPTER 9

Effectively and Efficiently Instructing the Learner

We cannot teach people anything;
we can only help them discover
it within themselves.

—Galileo Galilei

A s described in chapter 8, instructing the learner involves a focus on knowledge and the processes of the cognitive system. These are necessary functions of a robust education system. Knowledge is important for success in the complex present and future world students must deal with, as are the skills of the cognitive system.

Conveying knowledge has always been important in U.S. education. More recently, the processes of the cognitive system have been emphasized. But if we are to provide opportunities to awaken the learner in a systematic fashion, we must become more efficient at instructing the learner. This can be accomplished in two ways:

1. Decrease the amount of time directly teaching knowledge.

2. Increase the amount of time directly teaching cognitive skills.

Decrease the Amount of Time Directly Teaching Knowledge

One of the biggest changes that should occur immediately in K–12 education is to decrease the amount of time directly teaching knowledge. Virtually every school in the United States is attempting to provide instruction in a vast amount of content mandated (or at least strongly suggested) by forces outside of its local communities. These forces have historical roots in what can be called the "standards movement" in U.S. education.

The standards movement in the United States began in 1989 when President George H. W. Bush convened an Education Summit in Charlottesville, Virginia, that included the state governors (Marzano & Haystead, 2008). One byproduct of that summit was six educational goals. One of those goals was that "all children will leave grades four, eight, and twelve having demonstrated competency in challenging subject matter" (Rothman, 2011, p. 30).

Recognizing that the federal government did not have the expertise internally to identify that "challenging subject matter," the Bush administration issued grants to subject-matter professional organizations to identify the essential content students needed to know and, by default, articulate a tacit curriculum that would be employed across the country. The National Council of Teachers of Mathematics (NCTM) led the way, and soon standards were also established for English language arts, science, social studies, history, civics, government, geography, foreign languages, business, health, physical education, technology, and the arts (dance, theater, visual arts, and music). In 1994, the reauthorization of the Elementary and Secondary Education Act (ESEA) required all states to "develop challenging standards for student performance in at least mathematics and English language arts and assessments to measure that performance against the standards" (Rothman, 2011, p. 42). This made the tacit curriculum established by the national standards a concrete mandate, at least in mathematics and English language arts. The mandate was made salient when President George W. Bush signed the No Child Left Behind (NCLB) legislation.

While the growing trend toward mandated standards certainly seemed like a step in the right direction, it soon became evident that far too many standards had been identified, and therefore, far too much content had to be taught. To illustrate, in 1999 John Kendall and Robert Marzano identified two hundred separate standards and 3,093 benchmarks in the standards documents created as a result of the Education Summit in 1989. Marzano and Kendall estimated that it would take teachers 15,465 hours to cover all of them. They also estimated that teachers had only 9,042 hours of instructional time available to them across grades K–12. In effect, the mandated content could not be taught in the time available to teachers. These findings led Marzano and Kendall to conclude that "the answer to the question of whether the standards documents considered as a group contain too much content from an instructional perspective . . . is an unqualified 'yes'" (p. 104). More recently, the standards movement took another turn.

In 2009, the National Governors Association Center for Best Practices (NGA) and the Council of Chief State School Officers (CCSSO) agreed to take part in "a state-led process that will draw on evidence and lead to development and adoption of a common core of state standards . . . in English language arts and mathematics for grades K–12" (as cited in Rothman, 2011, p. 62). To date, these Common Core State Standards (CCSS) have been adopted or adapted in the vast majority of states. Although one of the goals of this effort was to decrease the amount of content in the standards, there are still profound problems with the amount of content to be taught and the time available to students (see Marzano, Yanoski, Hoegh, & Simms, 2013, for a discussion).

How can we alleviate the problem of a bloated, knowledge-based curriculum? The simple answer is that more trimming is needed. In a series of works, Marzano and colleagues (Marzano, 2003b, 2006; Marzano et al., 2013) have called for parsing the knowledge embedded in the standards into content that is *essential* and content that is *supplemental*. The essential content should be parsimonious and focused enough to allow teachers time to go into depth on topics as opposed to simply "covering" those topics at a surface level. Indeed, over the last few decades, countries that tend to outperform the United States on assessments of students' content knowledge tend to teach less content but in far greater depth (see Marzano, 2003b, for a discussion). In chapter 12, we consider how such a parsing might be accomplished. Briefly though, schools and districts are responsible for trimming the amount of content teachers are expected to explicitly address. This is done by identifying specific information and skills that are critical at each grade level and monitoring students' status and growth in these critical elements.

Increase the Amount of Time Directly Teaching Cognitive Skills

While the skills of the cognitive system have always been employed to a certain extent, in recent years they have been elevated to a more prominent and visible role, particularly through the CCSS. Specifically, in addition to articulating more rigorous content in mathematics and English language arts (ELA) that will enhance the knowledge base of U.S. students, the CCSS also identified cognitive skills that can be directly taught to students and then used to apply mathematics and ELA content in meaningful ways. These skills are embedded in what are referred to as the Standards for Mathematical Practice and the college and career readiness anchor standards.

Marzano and colleagues (2013) identified ten cognitive skills from the CCSS that can be applied not only to mathematics and

ELA but also to virtually every subject area. These are listed and briefly described in table 9.1 on pages 112–113.

Table 9.1 also provides signal words a teacher might use to cue students that a particular skill is required at a particular time. For example, the following signal words and phrases cue students that decision making is the appropriate skill to use for a given task:

- Decide
- Select the best among the following alternatives
- Which among the following would be the best
- What is the best way
- Which of these is most suitable

It is important that teachers provide direct instruction regarding the nature of these cognitive skills and the steps involved in their execution. This is necessary to ensure that the cognitive skills are executed rigorously by students so they might derive maximum value from their use. When these cognitive skills are taught explicitly, they allow students and teachers to cycle through content, challenge it, and refine it. Addressed in this way, content in any field becomes "a landscape that is explored by criss-crossing it in many directions" (Spiro, Vispoel, Schmitz, Samarapungavan, & Boerger, 1987, p. 178).

In the next sections, we consider how direct instruction might be carried out for two of the ten cognitive skills listed in table 9.1. For a more detailed discussion of all ten cognitive skills, see *Using Common Core Standards to Enhance Classroom Instruction & Assessment* (Marzano et al., 2013) and *Teaching & Assessing 21st Century Skills* (Marzano & Heflebower, 2012).

Generating Conclusions

Human beings are constantly generating conclusions about the things they see, hear, read, and experience in a variety of

Table 9.1: Cognitive Skills From the Common Core State Standards

Cognitive Skills	Description	Signal Words and Phrases
Generating Conclusions	Involves combining pieces of known information to form new ideas	Generalize, what conclusions can be drawn, what inferences can be made, create a generalization, create a principle, create a rule, trace the development of
Identifying Common Logical Errors	Involves analyzing information to determine how true it is	Identify errors, identify problems, identify issues, identify misunderstandings, assess, critique, diagnose, evaluate, edit, revise
Presenting and Supporting Claims	Involves expressing a new idea and presenting information to support it	Make and defend, predict, judge, deduce, what would have to happen, develop an argument for, under what conditions
Navigating Digital Sources	Involves using electronic resources to find credible and relevant information	What are you looking for, what is the best way to find, skim or read closely, assess the relevance of, assess the credibility of, other sources, other points of view
Problem Solving	Involves accomplishing a goal in spite of obstacles or limiting conditions	Solve, how would you overcome, adapt, develop a strategy to, figure out a way to, how will you reach your goal under these conditions

Decision Making	Involves using criteria to select among alternatives that initially appear to be equal	*Decide, select the best among the following alternatives, which among the following would be the best, what is the best way, which of these is most suitable*
Experimenting	Involves generating and testing explanations of observed phenomena	*Experiment, generate and test, test the idea that, what would happen if, how would you test that, how would you determine if, how can this be explained, based on the experiment, what can be predicted*
Investigating	Involves identifying confusions or contradictions about ideas or events and suggesting ways to resolve those confusions or contradictions	*Investigate, research, find out about, take a position on, what are the differing features of, how did this happen, why did this happen, what would have happened if*
Identifying Basic Relationships Between Ideas	Involves consciously analyzing relationships between ideas to better understand complex texts	*Categorize, compare and contrast, give an example, restate, differentiate, discriminate, distinguish, summarize, sort, what was the cause of, what is the relationship between, infer, create an analogy, create a metaphor, classify, organize, what was the result of, identify a broader category, identify categories, identify reasons, identify different types, sequence*
Generating and Manipulating Mental Images	Involves creating images in one's mind to facilitate deep processing and memory of information	*Symbolize, depict, represent, illustrate, draw, show, use models, diagram, chart, describe the key parts of, describe the relationship between*

Source: Adapted from Marzano et al., 2013.

ways. Many (if not most) of the thoughts we have during these experiences are inferences formed from premises. To illustrate, consider a student who is watching a football game and sees an interview with the quarterback from one of the teams. The student thinks, "He must be rich." Another student who sees the previews for an animated feature film thinks, "Only young children and their parents will see this movie." Both of these conclusions are based on premises.

Consider the first conclusion about the quarterback: "He must be rich." The premises underlying the conclusion might be stated as:

> Foundational premise: All star football quarterbacks are rich.
> Minor premise: He is a star quarterback.
> Conclusion: He must be rich.

The premises underlying the conclusion about the animated movie might be stated as:

> Foundational premise: Only young children and their parents go to see animated movies.
> Minor premise: This is an animated movie.
> Conclusion: Only young children and their parents will see this movie.

The vast majority of conclusions formed by human beings on a moment-by-moment basis can be represented or parsed as shown here. When forming conclusions, we start with a foundational premise we believe to be true ("All star quarterbacks are rich" or "Only young children and their parents go to see animated movies"). We also generate a minor premise about something we have just experienced (that is, "He is a star quarterback" or "This is an animated movie"). Based on the relationship between the foundational premise and the minor premise, which we generated from a recent experience, we form a conclusion ("He must be rich" or "Only young children and their parents will see this movie").

This basic understanding of how the human mind operates when forming such conclusions is a potentially powerful awareness in the hands of students because it provides them with a lens through which to see how they think, as well as how other people think (even those with whom they disagree). To this end, students can be led to realize that a conclusion can be logical or valid but untrue because one or more of the premises are untrue. For example, consider the following premises and accompanying conclusion:

> Foundational premise: Men are not very sensitive.
> Minor premise: Bob is a man.
> Conclusion: Bob is not very sensitive.

Based on the foundational premise and the minor premise, the conclusion that "Bob is not very sensitive" is logical (or, in technical terms, *valid*). However, the conclusion is untrue because the foundational premise is not true; that is, it is not true that all men are not very sensitive. This is the ultimate goal of teaching students about conclusions—providing them with the tools to vet conclusions for their validity and truth. With this skill under their control, students can excavate the logic underlying great ideas and destructive ideas alike.

The process of vetting a conclusion can be applied to historical events, current events, and events in students' individual lives. To illustrate the use of this process with historical events, consider a high school teacher I encountered a number of years ago. After teaching his students about the relationship between premises and conclusions, this teacher had students examine primary documents from the Nazi regime (for example, sections of Adolf Hitler's book *Mein Kampf*) to identify foundational and minor premises members of the Nazi party might have had. With these premises listed on chart paper, students generated conclusions that would logically (that is, validly) follow if one started with those premises. The students found that certain heinous conclusions Nazis had come to—like the necessity to exterminate the Jewish people—were, in fact, logical or valid. However, these valid conclusions were untrue because the premises they were based on were untrue (for example, the existence of a master race). The overall conclusion the students came to was that the heart of prejudicial thinking is valid reasoning from untrue premises. Quite obviously, this is a powerful conclusion for students to generate of their own accord.

To illustrate the use of vetting conclusions with current events, a teacher I met had students identify conclusions and the supporting premises of President Obama and candidate Mitt Romney during one of the debates of the 2012 presidential election. Students found that both candidates expressed at least some conclusions that were logical or valid but most probably untrue because they were based on faulty premises.

Finally, to illustrate the process of vetting conclusions in students' personal lives, a psychology teacher had students examine conclusions they had formed about important people in their lives (such as members of their family). Students reported that many of their negative conclusions about people were based on premises that were faulty—again, a very powerful and potentially transformative observation on their part.

Problem Solving

The ability to solve problems has been cited in the literature with regard to its importance in the K–12 curriculum (Anderson, 1983; Frederiksen, 1984; Rowe, 1985; van Dijk & Kintsch, 1983; Wickelgren, 1974). Over the years, Marzano and colleagues have developed a number of models for effective teaching of problem solving (Marzano, 2007; Marzano et al., 1988; Marzano, Paynter, & Doty, 2003; Marzano & Pickering, 1997). Problem solving has significant application in day-to-day life as well as the world of academics.

One of the first things students should know about problem solving is what it means to have a problem. Technically speaking, a problem occurs when there is a goal and obstacles or constraints in the way of attaining that goal. To illustrate, assume that a student wakes up in the morning and realizes she has overslept. This situation is clearly problematic. There is a goal to get to school on time. There is an obstacle in that the amount of time is severely limited from what is usually available. Another example of a problem is when a student realizes she has forgotten her homework for a specific class. The goal is to turn in the homework on time. The obstacle is that she doesn't have the homework, and constraints might include not having a cell phone or knowing that no one is at home who could bring it to her at school. Still another example is a situation in which a student wants to go the school's football game on Friday night but doesn't have a car and can't get a ride from his parents. The goal is to go to the football game. The obstacle is that he doesn't have a means of transportation. Constraints might include his curfew or rules his parents have set about riding in friends' cars.

Students' awareness of the nature of a problem provides the foundation for them to understand and employ a strategy for solving problems. Table 9.2 (page 118) depicts a problem-solving strategy that can be taught to students and adapted to a variety of situations and problem types. Each step in table 9.2 should be exemplified and discussed with students.

Step 1 introduces the concept of determining whether you really have a problem when you encounter an obstacle to a goal. In some cases, the immediate goal might not be very important. For example, if your goal is to go to a movie tonight but you don't have enough money, you are involved in a problem situation—at least on the surface. A goal exists (go to the movie tonight) and an obstacle or constraint is in the way (you don't have enough money to go). But going to a movie on a particular night is of little consequence in the grand scheme of things. Consequently, the detailed and potentially stressful process of problem solving might not be worth the effort to achieve this rather inconsequential goal.

Table 9.2: A Problem-Solving Strategy

Step 1	Identify the goal you are trying to achieve, and then determine whether you actually have a problem by asking, "Is the goal truly important to me, or is it something that I can ignore?"
Step 2	If you determine that you actually have a problem, take a moment to affirm the following: • There are probably many ways available to me to solve this problem. • Help is available to me if I look for it. • I am capable of solving this problem if I'm willing to work at it.
Step 3	Identify what is missing by describing the obstacle in your way or the constraints on what you can do. Identify possible solutions for replacing what is missing or for overcoming the obstacle.
Step 4	For each of the possible solutions you have identified, determine how likely it is to succeed. Consider the resources each solution requires and how accessible they are. Consider the help you might need to attain the resources.
Step 5	Try out the solution you believe has the greatest chance of success and fits your comfort level for risk.
Step 6	If your solution doesn't work, go back to another solution and try it out.
Step 7	If no solution can be found that works, "revalue" what you are trying to accomplish by looking for a more basic goal that can be accomplished.

This first step is intended to make students aware of the fact that not all problems are worth the energy and time it takes to solve them. Throughout their lives, there might be times when it is better to accept the current situation and use their energies and resources on more important issues.

Step 2 addresses the negative self-talk that commonly occurs whenever a problem is at hand. Although self-talk is a natural occurrence, negative self-talk can have a profound effect on one's ability to solve problems. Students can overcome this tendency by replacing negative self-talk with positive self-talk. In step 2, students are encouraged to affirm useful beliefs, such as:

- There are a number of ways to solve the problem.

- Help is probably available.

- Students can solve the problem if they are willing to work at it.

These phrases (and others like them) help students cultivate a positive attitude when confronted with problems.

Step 3 prompts students to clarify the obstacles or constraints that are in the way of accomplishing the goal. The clearer they can be about obstacles and constraints, the more able they are to identify solutions. At the completion of step 3, students should have a list of possible solutions that are tied to specific obstacles or constraints.

Step 4 addresses the critical issue of availability of resources necessary to enact solutions. Where a specific solution might directly address the obstacle or constraint in the way, it might not be readily accessible. This step also introduces the concept of seeking help. This is particularly important when it is hard to attain resources for promising solutions.

Step 5 prompts students to select the solution that has the best chance of success. This determination includes whether the resources necessary to execute the solution are available. This step also introduces the concept of risk. Some possible solutions might have a good chance of succeeding but carry a fair amount of risk. In fact, some solutions might be so risky that they aren't worth trying.

Step 6 directs students to continually monitor how well their selected solution is working. If it is clear that it has failed or is failing, the student will then select another solution. In effect, the sixth step helps students understand that effective problem solving is sometimes an iterative process of trying possible solutions until one eventually works.

Step 7 introduces the rather revolutionary concept of *revaluing*. This is a strategy effective problem solvers use when no direct solution can be found. Revaluing involves identifying a goal that can be reached when the original goal of the problem-solving process cannot. To illustrate, assume that someone had a goal of flying home to see his relatives on Christmas Eve to attend the traditional family pre-Christmas celebration, as well as the celebration on Christmas Day. However, upon arrival at the airport, he found that his flight had been cancelled. After an exhaustive search of possible flights, it was clear that none would get him home on time. The individual then revalued the situation. He found a flight leaving at 6:00 the next morning that would get him home in plenty of time for the Christmas Day celebration. He also found a hotel near the airport with a strong Internet connection. He checked in at the hotel and used Skype to virtually participate in the Christmas Eve activities. While his original goal was to participate in the Christmas Eve and Christmas Day activities in person, his revalued goal was to participate virtually in the Christmas Eve celebration and in person during the Christmas Day celebration. Revaluing turns unsolved problems into at least partially solved problems.

Teachers can use this process (or parts of it) to examine problems encountered in history, literature, current events, and so on. For example, consider step 5, which deals with trying out a solution that fits one's personal tolerance for risk. If students were reading a book from the *Harry Potter* series by J. K. Rowling, the teacher might ask them to identify a problem that Harry, Ron, and Hermione encounter, possible solutions for the problem, and the level of risk associated with each solution. The teacher might then ask students to examine which solution the protagonists chose in the story and what their choice reveals about each character's risk tolerance.

For example, at the end of *Harry Potter and the Sorcerer's Stone*, a magical stone is missing and the antagonist, Voldemort, is seeking it. The problem is that Voldemort might find the stone and use it for his evil ends. To solve the problem, Harry, Ron, and Hermione decide to sneak into a forbidden area of Hogwarts to try to find the stone before Voldemort does. Harry is almost killed in the process. Students might first list all the possible solutions Harry and his friends could have tried, as well as each solution's level of risk. They could then examine the protagonists' discussion and final decision about which solution to try, determining through their discussion that Harry has a rather high tolerance for risk. The teacher can then ask students to compare Harry's level of risk tolerance to their own and explain what solution they would have chosen in the same situation.

Alternatively, students might study an event in history, such as the launch of the space shuttle *Challenger*. Students could examine the problem NASA faced on the morning scheduled for the shuttle's launch: temperatures were lower than expected. They could generate possible solutions for the problem and assign a level of risk to each one. For example, students might determine that the risk associated with launching the shuttle in colder temperatures was too high for the solution to be acceptable; the cold temperatures threatened the structural integrity of the O-rings on the rocket's boosters, there was no backup system if the O-rings failed, and the failure of the O-rings would endanger the lives of the crew. Students could examine alternative solutions generated by NASA, generate alternative solutions themselves, assign a level of risk to each solution, and identify less risky (but still acceptable) solutions that NASA might have chosen.

Finally, if students examine a current event, such as the Arab Spring, they might study a problem faced by President Obama: how should the United States respond to the violence and uprisings in Egypt, Syria, and other Middle Eastern and North African countries? Students could generate solutions to the problem and assign a level of risk to each. They might decide that one solution was for the United States to declare war on countries that oppressed or persecuted their own citizens. They might decide the solution was risky for several reasons: the threat of political unpopularity, the uncertain nature of intelligence (making it difficult to decide exactly which countries were oppressing or persecuting their citizens), and the logistical challenges of combat in the Middle East and North Africa.

Of course, the problem-solving strategy can and should also be used by students to examine problems in their own lives. An elementary teacher once described to me how students applied the strategy to problems they encountered in school—particularly from the perspective of step 3 (identifying obstacles or constraints). Students reported that viewing problems from this perspective provided a clarity they had not experienced before. A secondary teacher asked students to examine problems in their lives from the perspective of step 7 (revaluing). Many students reported that they had not thought of the step as an option, and doing so helped them approach problems with less anxiety.

Tightening and Focusing the Current System

Instructing the learner is a necessary part of an effective K–12 system of education. It must be done effectively and efficiently. This means we must tighten the current system and focus our energies and resources. In this chapter, we have outlined two important initiatives to this end: decrease the amount of time directly teaching knowledge and increase the amount of time directly teaching cognitive skills. These actions, done efficiently, help provide an opportunity to awaken the learner.

CHAPTER 10

Laying the Foundation to Awaken the Learner

*It is the supreme art of the
teacher to awaken joy in creative
expression and knowledge.*

—Albert Einstein

To awaken the learner, students must be made aware of the processes of the self-system and the metacognitive system. Although rare, addressing the self- and metacognitive systems is not a brand-new concept. Indeed, the idea of teaching students about these systems was discussed over twenty years ago within the context of *conative skills*. Specifically, Richard Snow and Douglas Jackson (1993) referred to conative skills as the intersection of the mental powers of the cognitive system, beliefs, and emotions. In a number of works, McCombs alluded to conative skills as the intersection of skill and will (McCombs, 1984, 1986, 1989; McCombs & Marzano, 1990). Others have referred to the importance of teaching to the self- and metacognitive systems without necessarily using the term *conative*. For example, Daniel Goleman (1995) noted that people are well served when they cultivate "a neutral mode that maintains self-reflectiveness even amidst turbulent emotions" (p. 47). Robert Marzano and Tammy Heflebower (2012) used the phrase "understanding and controlling oneself" (p. 121).

Our discussion of the conative skills that are central to awakening the learner begins with the curriculum of the self-system.

The Curriculum of the Self-System

Being aware of the self-system has the potential to put students in control of their thoughts and actions, perhaps more than any other form of acquired knowledge. This is because the self-system is central to human functioning. As Mihaly Csikszentmihalyi (1990) explained:

> The self is no ordinary piece of information. . . . In fact, it contains [almost] everything . . . that has passed through consciousness: all the memories, actions, desires, pleasures, and pains are included in it. And more than anything else, the self represents the hierarchy of goals that we have built up, bit by bit, over the years. . . . At any given time, we are usually aware of only a tiny part of it. (p. 34)

The curriculum of self-system would focus on at least three factors: scripts, interpretations, and basic operating principles.

Scripts

Probably one of the more powerful constructs in terms of explaining human behavior is the concept of the *scripts*. Scripts were first popularized by Roger Schank and Robert Abelson (1977) as internal structures that articulate specific actions to be taken in specific situations. Teun van Dijk (1980) further explained that scripts have prototypical components (components that are always executed when engaged in a specific activity) and free components (components that might be executed in a specific situation but are not necessary to accomplishing a specific goal in that situation). To illustrate the structure of a script, consider the paraphrase of Schank and Abelson's (1977) restaurant script depicted in table 10.1.

Table 10.1: The Restaurant Script

Roles	Customer, waitress, chef, cashier
Reason	To get food so as to go up in pleasure and down in hunger
Scene 1: Entering	<ul><li>Enter restaurant.</li><li>Find empty table.</li><li>Sit at empty table.</li></ul>
Scene 2: Ordering	<ul><li>Receive menu.</li><li>Read menu.</li><li>Decide what to eat.</li><li>Give order to server.</li></ul>
Scene 3: Eating	<ul><li>Receive food.</li><li>Eat food.</li><li>Engage in pleasant conversation while eating if accompanied by others.</li></ul>
Scene 4: Exiting	<ul><li>Ask for check.</li><li>Receive check.</li><li>Pay check, and tip server.</li><li>Leave restaurant.</li></ul>

Table 10.1 depicts the prototypical components (those that will always be executed) when frequenting a restaurant—you enter the restaurant, find an empty table, examine the menu, and so on. Free components might include having light, friendly conversations with the server or restaurant manager. Human beings have tens of thousands of scripts for even the most specific of actions, such as brushing teeth, taking the garbage out, and so on.

At a very basic level, students can be made aware that they have scripts. This notion can be introduced by asking them to identify the routines they have in their lives—things they do the same way every day. Students will quite naturally be guided to identify scripts like getting ready for school, going to lunch, and so on. A discussion about the importance of routines or scripts should also occur, with an eye toward demonstrating that scripts make us more efficient. However, the discussion should also help illuminate the fact that interacting with people or challenging situations using scripts can make us inattentive and less sensitive than we might otherwise be. For example, always interacting with siblings the same way when they do certain things we don't like lessens our attentiveness to what is actually occurring at the moment and lessens our sensitivity to possible needs of our sibling. Students should be guided to the ultimate realization that scripts, while necessary and useful in our lives, can also close us off to possibilities that might come our way.

Interpretations

As we have seen, an individual chooses to engage in a new task or situation based on his or her interpretation of that task or situation. The process of forming an interpretation about a new task or situation involves four major components: (1) how a person classifies it, (2) how important the person believes it is, (3) the extent to which a person believes he or she can be successful at it, and (4) a person's emotional response to it. One might say that a person will engage in a new task or situation based on his or her answers to the following four questions:

- What is it?

- How important is it?

- Can I be successful at it?

- How do I feel about it?

A curriculum designed to awaken the learner would necessarily teach students about this working dynamic of the self-system. We consider important aspects for each of these four elements.

What Is It?

This first question deals with how an individual classifies a new task or situation. For example, a student in a social studies class who views learning about the U.S. Senate as "another chore you have to do in this class" will react one way. Another student who interprets it as "an opportunity to add to my knowledge base" will react a different way.

Carolyn Mervis (1980) explained that classifying is an essential aspect of human thinking, simply because we can't afford to react to every event or experience as if it was new. Rather, over the course of our lives we learn how to react to events that we classify the same way. We see an elderly lady trying to change a flat tire on the road, and we classify that as a situation where someone needs assistance. We observe a young child trying to reach for something above her head, and we classify it the same way. In both cases, we move into our helping scripts, even though the specific type of help we provide is different in the two situations. Our ability and propensity to classify the world around us allow us to make sense of that world.

Classification is the mechanism that allows humans to make sense of the world, but this fundamental human trait is both a blessing and a curse. Robert Marzano and Jana Marzano (2010) explained that it is a blessing in that it affords human beings the power to interpret (quickly and efficiently) almost anything with which they come into contact. It is a curse in the sense that once we have classified something, our reaction is set in place. For example, once we classify a new person we have met as a "bore," our reaction to that person is relatively set. This is because we begin executing our script for boring people. Obviously, the concept of scripts and the innate process of classification can and should be linked. Once we classify someone or something, we execute one or more scripts based on our classification. Again, while this makes us more efficient, it might also limit the possibilities available to us.

How Important Is It?

The answer to the question regarding the importance of a new task or situation is determined by an individual's system of goals.

Specifically, Marzano and Marzano (1988, 2010) contended that at any point in time, an individual is executing a *situated goal* (or pursuing a desired outcome) that relates to a *specific goal*. The specific goal relates to a *general goal*, which itself probably relates to a *basic operating principle*. This is depicted in figure 10.1.

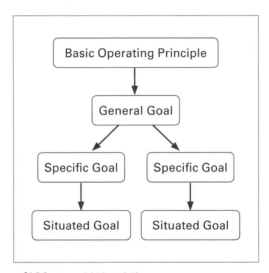

Source: Marzano & Marzano, 2010, p. 348.

Figure 10.1: Basic operating principles and goals.

According to figure 10.1, human beings judge the importance of new tasks and situations from the perspective of a hierarchic structure that includes situated goals, specific goals, general goals, and basic operating principles. To understand this structure, it is useful to start at the top with basic operating principles.

A *basic operating principle* is a premise someone has about the nature of the world and how he or she fits within it. For example, a student's basic operating principle could be that "you succeed in life if people who are popular like you." Under this basic operating principle, the student will have a *general goal* to get as many popular people as possible to like him. Under this general goal, he would have a more *specific goal*, such as getting all the popular athletes at school and all the popular youth at his church to like him. *Situated goals* come into play whenever the student is in a situation that has the potential of advancing one or more of his general goals. For example, if the student goes to church and notices a youth member of the church who is popular, the student might set a situated goal to talk to the other student after church and say something that impresses that student.

Can I Be Successful at It?

This question deals with a student's sense of self-efficacy. According to Dale Schunk and Frank Pajares (2009), "Self-efficacy refers to the perceived capabilities for learning or performing actions at designated levels" (p. 35). There are many ways that teachers can help students understand the concept of self-efficacy, including the work of Hazel Markus and her colleagues on possible selves (Cross & Markus, 1994; Markus & Nurius, 1986; Markus & Ruvolo, 1989) and the work of Martin Seligman on optimism (Seligman, 2006). Research that is most directly applicable to awakening the learner is that of self-theories by Carol Dweck and her colleagues (Dweck, 2000, 2006; Dweck & Master, 2009). Specifically, Dweck challenged the belief that the best way to motivate students is to boost their confidence:

> In elementary school, parents and teachers may constantly praise these children for how well they do, how smart they are, how quickly they learn. It might seem that these early successes would lay the foundation for a life of self-confidence and high academic achievement. Yet, many of these students struggle when they reach junior high school, and their grades begin to show a downward trajectory. . . . Suddenly classes are challenging, and hard work is necessary for success. How do students respond when the going gets tough? Do they remind themselves that they are intelligent and capable, roll up their sleeves, and get down to work? Unfortunately, many of them do not. Instead many choose to give up, to take the easy way out, and try to get by with the minimum amount of effort. Why does this happen and what can educators do? (Dweck & Master, 2009, p. 123)

In a series of studies, Carol Diener and Carol Dweck (1978) found that students can be sorted into one of two categories in terms of their responses to challenging situations. When presented with highly challenging tasks, students in one group blamed their lack of success on their abilities. They also sometimes expressed negative emotions through statements like, "This isn't fun" and "I don't like this anymore." Conversely, students in the other group remained more optimistic during challenging situations, expressing sentiments like, "I've almost got this" and "I like it when I can do something really hard."

Over time, Dweck and colleagues developed a powerful model of self-theories that could be used to explain a great deal of student behavior, particularly in challenging situations. Carol Dweck and Allison Master (2009) explained:

> Some students believe that intelligence is a fixed attribute [that is, the fixed mindset]. They believe they have only a certain amount and that's that. We call this an "entity theory." Students with an entity theory believe that intelligence is something fixed and unchanging. They believe that if individuals have a lot of it, then they are in good shape, but if they don't, there is not really anything they can do about it. Moreover, students with an entity theory may constantly worry about whether they have a lot or not. Other students see their intelligence as a changeable attribute, something that can be grown and strengthened over time [that is, the growth mindset]. We call this an "incremental theory." These students think that the more effort they put in, the more they will learn and the better their ability will be. These beliefs about intelligence have important implications for students. (p. 124)

Student motivation, particularly in the face of challenging tasks, is explained well from the perspective of self-theories. If students have a *fixed* mindset of human competence, they will tend to shrink from challenging tasks. But if they have a *growth* mindset, they will tend to embrace challenging situations. Robert Marzano and Debra Pickering (2011) described the defining characteristics of self-theories, as shown in table 10.2 (pages 132–133).

Simply teaching students that they have self-theories provides them with powerful ways to interpret their actions when challenges occur. A level up from understanding their self-theories, students can be led to experiment with changing their self-theories relative to specific situations. For example, a student who has a fixed mindset about his ability to do well at mathematics might try to cultivate a growth mindset regarding this subject by taking the position that putting effort into learning mathematics will eventually result in a sound understanding of the subject matter.

How Do I Feel About It?

The fourth question that affects a student's interpretation of a new task or situation deals with a student's emotional state at any point in time. Emotions play a central part in our experience from moment to moment. Reinhard Pekrun (2009) noted that human emotions have a profound impact on a wide variety of human behaviors. This in itself is a powerful awareness to provide to students. Their feelings about an event have a tremendous influence on how they interpret that event. Thomas Gilovich (1991) explained that the automatic links made between classifications of new tasks and situations and our affective responses create inherent biases in our interpretations, "biases that must be recognized and overcome if we are to arrive at sound judgments and valid beliefs" (p. 3).

Another awareness to provide students is that emotions—particularly negative ones like anger or sadness—tend to linger. For example, when a person loses his or her temper, it takes quite a while for that person's thinking to normalize and become more rational. Researchers typically label the initial event as an *emotion* and the lasting effects of it as a *mood*. Moods can last for hours or even days (Pert, 1997). Goleman (1995) explained that emotions

Table 10.2: Characteristics of Self-Theories

Self-theories are relatively stable.	Once a student has developed a self-theory, he or she tends to stay with this theory.
Self-theories can be specific to a domain.	For example, a student might have a fixed mindset regarding mathematics but a growth mindset regarding music.
Different self-theories lead to different goals.	When students have a fixed mindset regarding competence, they tend to pick tasks that will show off or highlight their perceived innate abilities. Getting good grades and demonstrating that they are smart come first for these students. Those with a growth mindset will seek goals that help them learn, since learning new skills will enhance their performance.
Different self-theories lead to different beliefs about the value of effort.	Students who hold a fixed mindset of human competence will tend to devalue effort. Ability is paramount. If a student has ability, he or she will perform well. If he or she doesn't, effort will not help much. In fact, fixed-mindset students tend to see effort as a negative characteristic. If you have to work hard to achieve, then you're not smart. Dweck and Master (2009) noted that "this may be precisely why many high-achieving students stop working when junior high school becomes difficult. . . . They have coasted along on low effort, showing how smart they are. Now, effort is required and they are not willing to take the risk. They would prefer to do poorly and be regarded as smart but lazy than to exert effort and feel inept" (p. 127).

Students with growth mindsets tend to believe that effort is not only useful but also a vital component of success.	These students tend to support statements like, "The harder you work at something, the better you will be at it."
Different self-theories foster different reactions to failure.	Students who have fixed mindsets desire success in school, and as long as they are successful, their theories may have little impact on their performance. However, once students begin to experience setbacks or begin to worry about their performance, their self-theory may start to work against them. To those who hold a fixed mindset, failure at a particular task is an indication of low ability, and when faced with failure, fixed-mindset students will ascribe their failure to things outside of their control ("I really don't like this subject"). Given that failure is connected with things out of their control, fixed-mindset students have little chance of getting better. By contrast, when a student with a growth mindset fails, it's an indication he or she didn't try hard enough. Where failure promotes little or no action for the fixed-mindset student, it stimulates new and more focused action in the growth-mindset student.

Source: Adapted from Marzano & Pickering, 2011.

like anger tend to trigger a two-part response from the brain. The first part involves a surge of energy, allowing the body's "fight or flight" mechanism to function, and usually only lasts for a few minutes. The second part, however, involves the creation of a "general tonic background of action readiness, which lasts much longer . . . keeping the emotional brain in special readiness for arousal, and becoming a foundation on which subsequent reactions can build with particular quickness" (p. 60). This explains why it is easier to become angry about something (for example, a relatively neutral question) if one is already angry about something else (for example, an insensitive comment from a friend or a difficult day at work). Factors such as sleepiness and hunger can exacerbate moods, making people even more susceptible to lingering negative emotions (Sylwester, 2000).

A final awareness to provide students about emotions is that they can be triggered by chemical imbalances. For example, an individual might experience a prolonged sense of sadness because of a chemical imbalance. Ronald Kotulak (1996) explained that sadness or even aggressive behaviors can be caused by "an imbalance of key neurotransmitters, such as serotonin and noradrenaline" (p. 88). Depression is caused by a deficit of the neurochemicals norepinephrine and serotonin (Amen, 1998) and can often be treated through medications that resolve the imbalance. Chemical imbalances that affect the emotions can also affect the body, inhibiting appetite and sleep (Seligman, 1993).

Controlling Interpretations

Based on the previous discussion, it is evident that people's interpretations of new tasks and situations dictate their thoughts and actions from that point on, until they are faced with a new task or situation. This occurs automatically without much conscious thought. Marzano and Marzano (2010) explained that human beings are "hardwired" to interact with the world around them but are often unaware of the dynamics of their interpretations and their effect on behavior: "Rather, for the most part, human beings are simply behaving in accordance with the rules that they have constructed about how to interpret events and how to react to events" (p. 354). Candace Pert (1997) explained from the perspective of the nervous system: "The nervous system is not capable of taking in everything, but can only scan the outer world for material that it is prepared to find by virtue of its wiring hookups, its own internal patterns, and its past experiences" (p. 147). While a certain amount of automaticity is necessary (in terms of interpreting the world around us), it is also important to develop the ability to control one's interpretations.

Marzano and Marzano (2010) recommended that once students understand the nature and power of interpretations, they ask the following questions when presented with new tasks and situations—particularly challenging ones:

- How am I interpreting this event?
- Does this interpretation help serve an important goal or an important principle in my life?
- If not, what is a more useful interpretation? (p. 356)

To illustrate how this protocol might be used, assume that in class, a student is presented with the opportunity to work with other students on a joint project for the next four class periods. Because the student doesn't like a few of the group members, she classifies this opportunity as a typical classroom task with which she must comply. She considers it of little importance except for the fact that she might get in trouble if she doesn't engage in it. She also thinks she doesn't have the type of personality to be very successful in situations like these. Finally, she simply doesn't feel very good about what the next week will be like.

Recognizing that she is agitated by the situation, she employs the protocol for examining new tasks and situations. The first question she was taught to ask herself is, "How am I interpreting this event?" She realizes that her interpretation of the event is being colored by her negative feelings toward some of the members of her group. The second question is, "Does this interpretation help serve an important goal or an important principle in my life?" Upon reflection, she realizes that this interpretation runs counter to at least two important goals she has for herself: to do well in the class and to be a positive person. Having examined her interpretation, she realizes that the negative feelings she is having toward her fellow group members are getting in her way. As she asks herself the final question—"If not, what is a more useful interpretation?"— she recognizes that she needs to reinterpret the situation. She realizes that she doesn't like certain members of her group simply because they aren't a part of her usual circle of friends. She chooses to reframe her initial reaction to those students. Instead of thinking, "I don't like them," she decides to think, "This is a great opportunity to get to know them." She examines her new interpretation and confirms that it will probably help make the next four class periods much more enjoyable.

Basic Operating Principles

A final aspect of the curriculum of the self-system is for students to focus on their basic operating principles. As mentioned previously in the discussion of the hierarchic structure of goals within the self-system (see figure 10.1, page 128), the driving structures in the hierarchy of goals are basic operating principles.

Basic operating principles lurk in the background of our consciousness. We are usually not thinking of them overtly, but they influence much of our thinking. They explain why we are drawn to do some things and not others. They even explain what inspires us to a great extent. For example, a student might be greatly inspired after watching a movie about an athlete who has overcome a debilitating injury from a car accident. The movie has provided evidence to the student that people can and do live their lives in accordance with the basic operating principle that "you can succeed even in the face of overwhelming odds." We are inspired when we are reminded that a basic operating principle we admire or aspire to is, in fact, valid.

Basic operating principles should certainly be fostered by students' parents and guardians. Specifically, the cultivation of some basic operating principles should be left to local families and church communities. For example, basic operating principles about the existence of God or an afterlife might be more appropriate for students to hear within their families (for a discussion, see Gaddy, Hall, & Marzano, 1996). There are many other basic operating principles that are appropriate to address in schools.

Using the work of Edward Deci and Richard Ryan (1987, 2008a, 2008b; Deci, 1995; Deci, Connell, & Ryan, 1989; Deci, Koestner, & Ryan, 1999; Ryan & Deci, 2000), we can identify three categories of basic operating principles that should be directly addressed in schools. Specifically, Deci (1995) identified three traits of a "fully functioning" (p. 88) individual: competence or effectiveness, autonomy or freedom, and relatedness.

Competence or Effectiveness

People who are fully functioning have experienced a sense of competence or effectiveness. In fact, Deci (1995) said the drive for competence and effectiveness is linked to intrinsic motivation:

> Feeling competent at the task is an important aspect of one's intrinsic satisfaction. The feeling of being effective is satisfying in its own right, and can even represent the primary draw for a lifelong career. People realize that the more they invest in a job, the better they will get at it, and thus the more intrinsic satisfaction they will experience. (p. 64)

This sense of competence or effectiveness is related to Dweck's concept of a growth mindset in which students are willing to take on challenging tasks. Deci explained further:

> The feeling of competence results when a person takes
> on and, in his or her own way, meets optimal challenges.
> Optimal challenge is a key concept here. Being able
> to do something that is trivially easy does not lead to
> perceived competence, for the feeling of being effective
> occurs spontaneously only when one has worked toward
> accomplishment. . . . All of us are striving for mastery, for
> affirmations of our own competence. One does not have to
> be best or first, or to get an 'A,' to feel competent; one need
> only take on a meaningful personal challenge and give it
> one's best. (1995, p. 66)

Essentially, people who feel competent and effective are intrinsically motivated and usually experience positive emotions when confronted with tasks that are challenging.

Autonomy or Freedom

A second trait of people who are fully functioning is that they operate from a sense of autonomy or freedom. As Deci (1995) noted:

> People who were asked to do a particular task but
> allowed the freedom of having some say in how to do it
> were more fully engaged by the activity—they enjoyed
> it more—than people who were not treated as unique
> individuals. (pp. 33–34)

Of course, the ability to act with complete autonomy or freedom is sometimes beyond the control of individuals. However, this awareness on the part of students might help guide their decisions in life so they seek out opportunities to engage in short- and long-term activities that provide them with autonomy and freedom.

Relatedness

The third characteristic of individuals who are fully functioning is that they experience a sense of relatedness. At first blush, it might seem that the trait of relatedness is inconsistent with the traits of autonomy or freedom. However, Deci (1995) noted that relatedness and autonomy are not incompatible:

> People have often portrayed the needs for autonomy and relatedness as being implicitly contradictory. You have to give up your autonomy, they say, to be related to others. But that is simply a misportrayal of the human being. Part of the confusion stems from equating autonomy and independence, which are in fact very different concepts. Independence means to do for yourself, to *not* rely on others for personal nourishment and emotional support. Autonomy, in contrast, means to act freely, with a sense of volition and choice. It is thus possible for a person to be independent and autonomous (i.e., to freely not rely on others), or to be independent and controlled (i.e., to feel forced not to rely on others). (pp. 88–89)

Relatedness is a desire to have a positive influence in the lives of other people. These people might be coworkers on a specific project or people who are positively affected by a project in which one engages.

Becoming Fully Functioning

As part of the curriculum of the self-system, students can be presented with the three traits of a fully-functioning individual as described by Deci (1995). They might also study the lives of famous people in history or current events for evidence of these traits.

At a more personal level, students can be asked to examine their own basic operating principles for evidence of these traits. Specifically, they might be asked to identify evidence that they operate from beliefs like the following:

- Life is more satisfying when you develop expertise at complex things (competence or effectiveness).

- Life is more satisfying when you use your unique skills and abilities and are willing to make independent decisions (autonomy or freedom).

- Life is more satisfying when you make the lives of other people better (relatedness).

This is a very introspective activity because it requires students to compare their behaviors with their beliefs. If a student has a basic operating principle that "life is more satisfying when you make the lives of other people better," we would expect to see evidence of this principle in his or her behavior. While this seems reasonable, Chris Argyris and Donald Schön (1974, 1978) have shown that there is often a discrepancy between a person's *espoused beliefs* and his or her *beliefs in action*. Stated differently, there is a difference between what people say they believe and what they actually do. For example, when asked, students might say they believe they should help other people less fortunate than themselves but have no evidence in their behavior of this belief. Marzano and Marzano (1988) explained this contradiction in the following way: a student might say she believes she should help other people (her espoused belief) but could actually have a contradictory basic operating principle (her belief in action) she is not aware of.

The Curriculum of the Metacognitive System

Teaching students about the metacognitive system is also an aspect of the conative skills identified by psychologists as important for success in life. The metacognitive system has been described in the research literature as responsible for monitoring, evaluating, and regulating the functioning of other types of thought (Brown, 1984; Flavell, 1978; Meichenbaum & Asarnow, 1979). The term *executive control* is commonly used to describe the major functions of the metacognitive system (Brown, 1978, 1980; Flavell, 1979, 1987; Sternberg, 1984, 1985, 1986a, 1986b). There are three aspects of the metacognitive system students should be made aware of: mindfulness, specifying goals, and process monitoring.

Mindfulness

At its core, metacognition involves being aware of what is occurring within us and around us at any moment. Ellen Langer (1989; Langer & Rodin, 1976; Langer & Weinman, 1981) has referred to this as *mindfulness*. Specifically, Langer (1989) explained that mindfulness involves a heightened sense of situational awareness and a conscious control over one's thoughts and behaviors relative to the situation. Marzano (2003a) further noted that:

> This frame of mind is not easy to cultivate and maintain because the human brain is predisposed to focus on a very narrow range of stimuli and to operate quite automatically relative to those stimuli. That is, we typically do not attend to all of what is happening around us. In fact, we commonly operate with very little conscious awareness of our environment, particularly regarding routine activities. (p. 65)

For the most part, operating with little conscious awareness of what is happening inside us and outside us is not problematic, but it does provide some humorous incidents in our lives. Langer (1989) related the following examples:

> Have you ever said "excuse me" to a store mannequin or written a check in January with the previous year's date? When in this mode, we take in and use limited signals from the world around us (the female form, the familiar face of the check) without letting other signals (the motionless pose, a calendar) penetrate as well. Once, in a small department store, I gave a cashier a new credit card. Noticing that I hadn't signed it, she handed it back to me to sign. Then she took my card, passed it through her machine, handed me the resulting form, and asked me to sign it. I did as I was told.

> The cashier then held the form next to the newly signed card
> to see if the signatures matched. (pp. 12–13)

Langer refers to such behavior as *mindlessness*, with the caveat that all of us engage in such behavior with few or no negative consequences. However, to develop mindfulness, it is necessary to practice operating from a heightened sense of awareness. As we have seen in the discussion of the self-system, one way to become aware of our interpretations of new tasks and situations is to ask the questions, "How am I interpreting this event?" "Does this interpretation help serve an important goal or an important principle in my life?" and "If not, what is a more useful interpretation?" The answers to these questions provide mindfulness relative to what is occurring *inside* us. There is an analogous set of questions that can help us become more mindful of what is happening *outside* of us. Such questions might include:

- Right now, who or what are my actions affecting?

- Are my actions affecting my environment in a positive or negative way?

- If my actions are having a negative effect, what should I stop doing or what should I start doing?

Students can practice using these questions (or adaptations of them) during the school day. A teacher once reported that upon asking themselves these questions, many students were surprised at how their actions in class, in the hallways, on the playground, and in the cafeteria were possibly affecting other students in a negative way. They were never aware of this possibility before.

Specifying Goals

Another aspect of employing the metacognitive system is to specify a clear goal when presented with a new task in which the learner has elected to engage. As Marzano and Kendall (2007) noted:

> One of the primary tasks of the metacognitive system is to establish clear goals. . . . It is the self-system that determines an individual's decision whether or not to engage in an activity. However, once the decision is made to engage, it is the metacognitive system that establishes a goal relative to that activity. . . . The goal-specifying function of the metacognitive system is responsible for establishing clear learning goals for specific types of knowledge. For example, it would be through the goal specification function of the metacognitive system that students would establish a specific goal or goals in terms of increasing their understanding or use of specific information presented in a mathematics class. (p. 54)

Being specific about a goal involves thinking about the characteristics of the end product when a goal is met. Once a clear end state is articulated, the student establishes a plan to reach that end state. Again, Marzano and Kendall (2007) noted:

> As part of the goal-specification process, an individual will usually identify what Hayes (1981) refers to as a clear end state—what the goal will look like when completed. This might also include the identification of milestones to be accomplished along the way. Last, it is the job of the goal specification function to develop a plan for accomplishing a given learning goal. This might include the resources that will be necessary and even timelines in which milestones and the end state will be accomplished. It is this type of thinking that has been described as strategic in nature (Paris, Lipson, & Wixson, 1983). (p. 54)

To illustrate the goal-specification process, consider a student who wants to do well in math class. Setting a specific goal involves clearly articulating what is necessary to do well; for example, the student might say to himself, "I'm going to learn how to do long division." To determine a clear end state, the student might ask his teacher to show him how to do a long division problem. As the student watches the teacher, he forms a picture of himself completing the same process. He realizes that he will need to accomplish three milestones along the way to his goal: (1) clearly identify the steps of the long division algorithm, (2) accurately subtract and multiply (since the algorithm requires those operations), and (3) learn a process for checking the answer. Finally, he develops a plan to accomplish his goal. He begins by writing down the steps of the long division algorithm and then uses his notes to practice on a set of problems the teacher gives him. He plays a math game on his iPad to practice subtraction and multiplication. He asks one of his friends to double-check his answers to division problems and observes the strategy his friend uses to check. He decides to use his friend's strategy to check his own answers.

Process Monitoring

Process monitoring involves continuously evaluating whether one's current actions are taking him or her closer to or farther away from the desired outcomes in a given situation. Marzano and Kendall (2007) described process monitoring in the following way:

> The process monitoring component of the metacognitive system typically monitors the effectiveness of a procedure being used in a task. For example, the metacognitive system will monitor how well the mental procedure of reading a bar graph or the physical procedure of shooting a free throw is being carried out. Quite obviously, the execution of a procedure is most effectively monitored when a goal has been set. Process monitoring also comes into play when a long-term or short-term goal has been established for information—for example, when a student has established the goal of better understanding polynomials. In this case, process monitoring addresses the extent to which that goal is being accomplished over time. (p. 54)

To illustrate the process-monitoring component of the metacognitive system, consider again the student with the goal to learn long division. As he works the set of practice problems using his notes about the long division algorithm, he stops every so often to make sure he isn't missing any steps. If he has missed one, he goes back and tries again, incorporating the missing step. As he practices subtraction and multiplication on his iPad, he monitors his score on the math game, trying to achieve 100 percent each time. As he uses his friend's strategy to check his answers, he pays attention to how often his answer is wrong and uses that information to refine his strategy.

Being Overt About the Conative Skills of the Self- and Metacognitive Systems

As we have seen, the self-system and metacognitive system have explicit awarenesses and processes that can be taught to students. Taken collectively, these awarenesses and processes are referred to as conative skills. Infusing the conative skills into the curriculum takes a conscious effort on the part of teachers and administrators. However, it is an effort with potentially big benefits. An understanding and control of the self- and metacognitive systems put students in a position to control their reactions to the environment and accomplish goals that are important to them. This can awaken in students a sense of personal efficacy that they might have never have had before.

There are specific activities that teachers and school leaders can engage in to create environments that both instruct and awaken learners. Chapter 11 discusses strategies teachers can use to balance these two elements in their classrooms. Chapter 12 outlines steps that school leaders can take to cultivate and strategically support a school- or districtwide focus on the self- and metacognitive systems.

CHAPTER 11

The Teacher Who Instructs and Awakens the Learner

*A teacher who is attempting to teach
without inspiring the pupil with a desire
to learn is hammering on cold iron.*

—Horace Mann

The previous chapters are intended to provide the teacher who seeks to instruct and awaken the learner with a blueprint as to how to accomplish both. To instruct the learner, the teacher focuses on knowledge and the cognitive system as depicted in the lower part of figure 8.1 (page 101) in chapter 8. This translates into a well-defined set of essential content that is parsimonious enough to be addressed with rigor and depth. Additionally, the teacher provides direct instruction in cognitive skills, as well as the opportunity for students to apply those skills.

To awaken the learner, the teacher provides students with an understanding of the skills of the self-system and metacognitive system as depicted in the upper part of figure 8.1. This involves addressing topics such as scripts, interpretations, basic operating principles, mindfulness, specifying goals, and process monitoring. The responsibility for instruction in these self-system and metacognitive elements would no doubt be spread out over multiple grade levels. For example, simple descriptions of concepts like scripts and interpretations could be provided in early grades and then gradually developed to more robust and nuanced concepts in later years.

In addition to teaching about the self-system and metacognitive system, the teacher who seeks to awaken the learner will engage in three types of activities in the classroom on a systematic basis:

1. Providing a positive emotional environment and inspiration for students

2. Providing opportunities for students to practice the conative skills of the self-system and metacognitive system

3. Engaging students in personal projects

Providing a Positive Emotional Environment and Inspiration for Students

As described in chapter 10, a student's emotional response to a situation is the gatekeeper to that student's willingness to engage in new tasks and situations. Teaching students about the nature of emotions and their influence on behavior will certainly give them some awareness and control over their emotional states. Additionally, there are many things a teacher can do to help create a positive emotional environment on a daily basis.

One of the most direct ways to establish a positive emotional environment is to ensure that all students believe they are accepted and supported. Stated differently, if students believe they are not accepted or supported, they will tend to have negative emotions. The relationship a student has with the teacher can go a long way to this end. Based on a series of studies, Carol Goodenow (1993) concluded that teacher support was consistently a good predictor of student motivation in middle school students. Kathryn Wentzel (2009) explained the importance of positive teacher-student relationships in the following way:

> Secure relationships are believed to foster children's curiosity and exploration of the environment, positive coping skills, and a mental representation of one's self as being worthy of love and of others being trustworthy. In contrast, insecure attachments are believed to result in either wary or inappropriately risky exploratory behavior, difficulty in regulating stress in new settings, and negative self-concepts. (p. 302)

Peer relationships are equally (if not more) important than teacher-student relationships. As noted by Gary Ladd, Sarah Herald-Brown, and Karen Kochel (2009):

> When peers dislike persons within their group, they tend to act in rejecting ways toward these children (e.g., ignoring, excluding them from activities), and these behaviors become observable indicators of rejection not only for rejected children, but also for the larger peer group. (p. 327)

Ladd and his colleagues went on to note that the longer students are rejected by peers, the less likely they are to participate in classroom activities. Additionally, students for whom a pattern of peer rejection was established in the elementary grades may establish their own pattern of profound disengagement in school.

Clearly, the teacher who seeks to awaken the learner should go to great lengths to ensure that all students feel accepted and supported by the teacher and their peers. Marzano and Pickering (2011) offered a number of strategies to this end, which are briefly summarized in table 11.1 (pages 150–151). For detailed discussions of these strategies, see *The Highly Engaged Classroom* (Marzano & Pickering, 2011).

Closely related to a positive emotional environment is an environment that inspires students. Recall that inspiration is directly related to basic operating principles. People become inspired when they see or hear of examples of people who have done great things by behaving in accord with their basic operating principles.

Table 11.1: Classroom Strategies That Enhance Teacher-Student and Peer Relationships

Fair and Equitable Treatment of All Students: Teachers can ensure that their classrooms are places where all students feel safe by curbing disruptive or hurtful behavior and letting students know that teachers will provide help to any student in need. Teachers can also help students have positive feelings about class by actively encouraging behavior that demonstrates respect. One way to accomplish this is to establish a set of basic rights in the classroom, such as "All students have the right to be treated with respect" or "All teachers have the right to be treated with respect."
Simple Courtesies: Teachers can make students feel welcome and acknowledged by greeting them at the door, calling them by their names, saying "Good morning," and so on. Making eye contact is a subtle but effective behavior to let students know you like and accept them. However, teachers should note that returning eye contact may be uncomfortable for some students, especially if they were taught that not making eye contact is the most respectful behavior. Teachers should adapt their use of simple courtesies to achieve the desired effects on students.
Physical Contact and Gestures: Teachers can demonstrate interest in and affection for a student through physical contact, such as giving a student a pat on the back. Of course, physical contact should always be used with attention to each student's age, gender, and culture (what may seem appropriate with one student might be inappropriate for another). Teachers can also use physical gestures (such as the OK hand signal, a thumbs-up, the touchdown sign, a wink, a nod, or a smile) to communicate affection for students. These make students feel good about themselves and the atmosphere of the classroom.
Students' Needs and Concerns: Teachers can display affection simply by attending to special needs students might have. While attending to certain students' needs (such as providing extra support to students with poor eyesight or learning disabilities) is required by law, students might also have more personal needs that teachers can take note of and make accommodations for. A student who has missed school because of a serious illness or a death in the family might need a little more support catching up than normal, or a student whose family has moved and has joined the class in the middle of the school year might need a bit more tutoring or emotional support than other students. Making accommodations for these types of needs sends the message that the teacher is concerned about the well-being of all students.

> **Positive Information About Students:** Teachers can communicate respect and acceptance by identifying something positive about students and using that information to plan instruction to address students interests and communicate concern for specific students. This is particularly true for students who have discipline issues or who appear alienated from the rest of the class or the teacher. Excellent ways to discover and use positive information about students include structured opportunities in class for students to share interests and accomplishments, conversations with parents and guardians, and conversations with fellow teachers.

Source: Adapted from Marzano & Pickering, 2011.

Unfortunately, in day-to-day life, students might not experience many examples of stories that inspire them. In fact, one could make the case that popular media provide little inspiration to students regarding the possibilities of their lives.

To counteract the potentially negative influence of popular media, teachers can make their classrooms places where students receive a steady diet of inspirational stories and quotations. In chapter 7, Darrell mentioned how *Aesop's Fables* and other tales and stories might be used. Contemporary examples of inspirational stories can also be employed. Marzano and Pickering (2011) provided the following example using the life of Roland Fryer:

> Roland Fryer was raised in Daytona Beach, Florida, in a tough, drug-infested urban neighborhood. With the support of his grandmother, he earned an athletic scholarship to the University of Texas. It was in college that he really began to excel. Not only did he graduate as a mathematics major, he also earned a PhD by the age of thirty and became a tenured professor at Harvard University. He was the youngest African American ever to have done so. He did not stop there, though. He created the Education Innovation Laboratory at Harvard, which specializes in research and development in the field of education. To improve the quality and rigor of education, he now partners with school districts to help administrators, teachers, and students understand

the factors affecting low performance in urban areas. He
even visits with students personally to encourage them to
invest in their own futures through education (Rhee, 2009).
(p. 128)

There are a number of resources teachers might use to gather
similar stories. Marzano and Pickering (2011) suggested the
following:

- *TIME* magazine online, www.time.com. *TIME* is famous
  for its personal profiles. This site even has a section
  where featured celebrities answer ten questions
  from an online audience. The yearly top-one hundred
  lists, such as the "100 Most Influential People," are
  inspirational personal story sources as well.

- *Kids With Courage: True Stories About Young People
  Making a Difference* by Barbara A. Lewis (1992). This
  book and others like it feature the personal stories of
  young people who faced many life obstacles, acted
  heroically in dangerous situations, or fought ambitiously
  for social or environmental causes.

- *It's Our World, Too! Stories of Young People Who Are
  Making a Difference* by Phillip M. Hoose (1993). This
  book offers personal stories and specific strategies for
  young people who want to become involved or make
  a difference but do not know how. For example, it has
  a chapter featuring ten tools for change—ten ways to
  help attract attention and begin to effect change.

- *Dare to Dream! 25 Extraordinary Lives* by Sandra
  McLeod Humphrey (2005). This book tells the brief
  biographies of twenty-five famous and influential
  people such as Abraham Lincoln, Maya Angelou, Jackie
  Robinson, and Eleanor Roosevelt. (p. 128)

Inspirational stories can also be provided by showing clips from movies such as *Rudy, A Beautiful Mind, October Sky, Oliver Twist, Mr. Holland's Opus, The Pursuit of Happyness, Apollo 13, Philadelphia, Babe,* and *Glory.*

Another way to promote an atmosphere of inspiration in the classroom is to systematically present students with quotes. Figure 11.1 provides selected quotes from Marzano and Pickering (2011) organized into five categories: (1) perseverance, (2) change, (3) greatness and following hopes and dreams, (4) opposition, and (5) optimism.

Perseverance

"Genius is 99 percent perspiration and 1 percent inspiration."
—Thomas A. Edison

"The man who can drive himself further once the effort gets painful is the man who will win." —Roger Bannister

"Without a struggle, there can be no progress." —Frederick Douglass

"Success seems to be largely a matter of hanging on after the others have let go." —William Feather

"When you get to the end of your rope, tie a knot and hang on."
—Franklin Delano Roosevelt

"I am always doing that which I cannot do, in order that I may learn how to do it." —Pablo Picasso

"Perseverance is failing nineteen times and succeeding the twentieth."
—Julie Andrews

"The difference between perseverance and obstinacy is that one comes from a strong will and the other from a strong won't."
—Henry Ward Beecher

"Ambition is the path to success. Perseverance is the vehicle you arrive in." —Bill Bradley

---

Source: Adapted from Marzano & Pickering, 2011, pp. 130–134.   Continued→

Figure 11.1: Quotations for inspiration.

"Most of the important things in the world have been accomplished by people who have kept on trying when there seemed to be no help at all." —Dale Carnegie

"History has demonstrated that the most notable winners usually encountered heartbreaking obstacles before they triumphed. They won because they refused to become discouraged by their defeats." —Bertie C. Forbes

"Perseverance is a great element of success. If you only knock long enough and loud enough at the gate, you are sure to wake up somebody." —Henry Wadsworth Longfellow

"It's not whether you get knocked down; it's whether you get up." —Vince Lombardi

"Success is going from failure to failure without a loss of enthusiasm." —Winston Churchill

Change

"Change is inevitable, growth is intentional." —Glenda Cloud

"Change does not roll in on the wheels of inevitability, but comes through continuous struggle. And so we must straighten our backs and work for our freedom. A man can't ride you unless your back is bent." —Martin Luther King Jr.

"They always say time changes things, but you actually have to change them yourself." —Andy Warhol

"The world is before you, and you need not take it or leave it as it was when you came in." —James Baldwin

"Never doubt that a small group of thoughtful, committed citizens can change the world. Indeed, it is the only thing that has." —Margaret Mead

"The chains of habit are too light to be felt until they are too heavy to be broken." —Warren Buffett

"If you want to truly understand something, try to change it." —Kurt Lewin

"Adapt or perish, now as ever, is nature's inexorable imperative." —H. G. Wells

"It is not possible to step into the same river twice." —Heraclitus

"To change is difficult. Not to change is fatal." —Ed Allen

Greatness and Following Hopes and Dreams

"I am the greatest; I said that even before I knew I was."
—Muhammad Ali

"The future belongs to those who believe in the beauty of their dreams."
—Eleanor Roosevelt

"There are those who look at things the way they are, and ask why. . . . I dream of things that never were, and ask why not?" —Robert Kennedy

"I've dreamt in my life dreams that have stayed with me ever after, and changed my ideas: they've gone through and through me, like wine through water, and altered the color of my mind." —Emily Brontë

"A man is not old until regrets take the place of dreams."
—John Barrymore

"Dream no small dreams for they have no power to move the hearts of men." —Johann Wolfgang von Goethe

"My dreams were all my own; I accounted for them to nobody; they were my refuge when annoyed—my dearest pleasure when free."
—Mary Shelley

"Imagination rules the world." —Napoleon Bonaparte

"Don't be afraid to see what you see." —Ronald Reagan

"You can't put a limit on anything. The more you dream, the further you get." —Michael Phelps

"History will be kind to me for I intend to write it." —Winston Churchill

"At the age of six I wanted to be a cook. At seven I wanted to be Napoleon. And my ambition has been growing ever since."
—Salvador Dalí

Opposition

"No one can make you feel inferior without your consent."
—Eleanor Roosevelt

"We must build dikes of courage to hold back the flood of fear."
—Martin Luther King Jr.

Continued→

"I used to think anyone doing anything weird was weird. Now I know that it is the people that call others weird that are weird."
—Paul McCartney

"If you break your neck, if you have nothing to eat, if your house is on fire, then you got a problem. Everything else is just inconvenience."
—Robert Fulghum

"Smooth seas do not make skillful sailors." —African proverb

"You cannot lead from the crowd." —Margaret Thatcher

"If my critics saw me walking over the Thames they would say it was because I couldn't swim." —Margaret Thatcher

"In the practice of tolerance, one's enemy is the best teacher."
—Tenzin Gyatso, Fourteenth Dalai Lama

"I've learned that you shouldn't go through life with a catcher's mitt on both hands; you need to be able to throw something back."
—Maya Angelou

"Everything negative—pressure, challenges—it's all an opportunity for me to rise." —Kobe Bryant

"Difficulty is the excuse history never accepts." —Edward R. Murrow

Optimism

"Don't worry about the world coming to an end today. It's already tomorrow in Australia." —Charles M. Schwab

"A pessimist is one who makes difficulties of his opportunities and an optimist is one who makes opportunities of his difficulties."
—Harry Truman

"In the long run, the pessimist may be proved right, but the optimist has a better time on the trip." —Daniel L. Reardon

"It's not the load that breaks you down, it's the way you carry it."
—Lena Horne

"There is hope for the future because God has a sense of humor, and we are funny to God." —Bill Cosby

"You cannot climb uphill by thinking downhill thoughts." —Anonymous

"Change your thoughts and you change the world." —Norman Vincent Peale

Providing Opportunities for Students to Practice the Conative Skills of the Self-System and Metacognitive System

In addition to building a positive emotional environment that promotes inspiration, teachers might look for opportunities to help develop students' awareness and control over their self-systems. This can be done in a variety of ways.

Provide Opportunities for Students to Discuss Possible Self-System Processes of Others

Once students have a basic understanding of self-system processes, they can be provided with opportunities to identify and analyze the self-system processes of others. This can easily be done using characters in a book they are reading. For example, while reading a story, students might analyze possible self-system processes of the main character. Questions presented to students to guide them in this endeavor could include:

- What type of script do you think the main character was operating from when he made that choice?

- What do you think was the basic operating principle behind the protagonist's actions when he acted in that way?

- How do you think the antagonist answered the question "What is it?" when he saw the protagonist's situation?

- How would you characterize the heroine's general emotional state when she decided to run away? How do you think that affected her actions?

To illustrate, consider the novel *The Secret Garden* by Frances Hodgson Burnett (1911/1987). Mary Lennox is an orphan sent to live with her uncle in England. Although she was an unpleasant, selfish, sickly child before, she gradually becomes strong, adventurous, and compassionate in her new surroundings. She discovers that she has a cousin, Colin Craven, and helps him undergo the same transformation that she herself has experienced—from a selfish invalid to a strong, happy, positive individual. After reading the story, the teacher could adapt the previously listed questions to help students examine the self-system processes of various characters. For example:

- What type of script do you think Mary was operating from when she was kind to Colin and told him stories?

- What do you think was the basic operating principle that caused Martha, Dickon, and Susan Sowerby to be kind to Mary?

- How do you think Mary answered the question "What is it?" when she found the key to the secret garden?

- How would you characterize Archibald Craven's general emotional state after his wife died? How do you think that affected his actions?

Questions like these can prompt students to analyze the self-systems of others, specifically the self-systems of characters in books they read.

Provide Opportunities for Students to Examine Their Own Self-System Processes Relative to Current Events

Students can also be asked to examine their own self-system processes. One way to facilitate this is to use high-visibility current events. For example, assume that the national news has reported the beaching of whales near San Diego. Teachers could ask students questions like the following (to help them examine their self-system processes relative to this event):

- Relative to this event, how did you answer the question "What is it?" (How did you classify this event?)

- How important do you think this event was? Why?

- Do you think you could do something about events like this? Please explain why.

- How did you feel about this event? Why?

Some students might answer the question "What is it?" by explaining that it is a tragedy; although one of the whales was saved and released back into the ocean, two of the whales died. When asked "How important do you think this event was?" some might say it was very important since the whales were humpbacks, an endangered species. In response to the question, "Do you think you could do something about events like this?" some students might respond by investigating causes of beaching and discover that the sonar used by naval and other governmental agencies may be responsible for whales becoming stranded. Students might decide that although they do not have a direct influence on the use of sonar, they could write letters to their state representatives in Congress and ask them to support legislation to limit the use of sonar in areas where whales typically live. Finally, students might articulate their feelings in response to the whale beachings. Although many students say that they feel sad, some students might feel motivated to learn more about whales and what they can do—beyond writing letters—to protect them.

Provide Opportunities for Students to Examine Their Own Self-System Processes Relative to Their Daily Lives

Finally, teachers could ask students to examine self-system processes as they relate to their daily lives. Specifically, teachers might ask students to identify common scripts they use when interacting with specific people or in specific situations. To illustrate, consider a student who has just learned that she will be required to complete a research project assignment in her English language arts class. Normally, the student would be overwhelmed by the project and therefore avoid it. However, having learned about her self-system and the human propensity to execute scripts, she recognizes that being overwhelmed is the first step of a script that does not help her achieve her goal of doing well in English class. Armed with that knowledge, she consciously chooses to change her script. Instead of feeling overwhelmed by the project and avoiding it, she makes an appointment with her English teacher. When they meet, the student employs a script she uses when she is trying to learn new things: she asks a question every so often and writes down the answer to the question. Although it takes some time, she finds that her new script helps her understand the project better and therefore not feel so overwhelmed by it.

Students might also be asked to examine their interpretations of significant events that have occurred in their lives. For example, after selecting something that has occurred recently in their lives, students could answer the following questions:

- Relative to this event, how did you answer the question "What is it?" (How did you classify this event?)

- How important do you think this event was? Why?

- Do you think you could do something about events like this? Please explain why.

- How did you feel about this event? Why?

A student who got into an argument with his sister on the way to school might examine it from the perspective of these questions. Thinking back, he realizes that when his sister wanted to listen to her radio station on the way to school, he classified the event as one in which she was getting her way, an occurrence he believes is all too common. It was a very important event to him, since he feels that she gets everything she wants because she is younger than he. He also realizes that he decided to do something about it, but instead of choosing to explain his point of view and seek a compromise, he got angry. He realizes he has negative feelings about the event because getting angry made his sister angry. Based on his analysis, he decides to at least stop and think about his interpretation before reacting in the future.

Engaging Students in Personal Projects

Personal projects are a perfect vehicle to engage students in the processes of the metacognitive system and reinforce many aspects of the self-system. Marzano and Pickering (2011) explained that personal projects are designed to provide students with opportunities to engage in projects that allow them to pursue goals that are highly important to them personally. To this extent, they help students become clearer about some of their basic operating principles and articulate and then pursue goals that are directly related to those principles. Additionally, personal projects allow students to employ the goal-setting and process-monitoring skills of the metacognitive system.

There are seven phases in a personal project, each one associated with a question or set of questions students must address. One useful feature of the seven phases is that teachers do not have to address them on a daily basis. Indeed, days or even weeks might separate phases to allow students time to complete the activities required in any given phase.

Phase One: What Do I Want to Accomplish?

A personal project begins with students selecting a personal goal. This goal should interest them and relate to a topic about which they are excited or passionate. One technique to help students select goals that truly inspire them is to pose the question, "What would you do if you knew you would not fail?" Of course, goal selection can be accompanied by a discussion about basic operating principles. Students might be reticent about sharing their goals or basic operating principles because they are concerned about being teased or ridiculed. The best way to address this is for teachers to engage in their own personal projects alongside students and share their responses during each phase. Students may also hesitate to share their goals because they do not believe that they can accomplish them. Such a situation invites a discussion of growth mindsets versus fixed mindsets.

Phase Two: Who Else Has Accomplished the Same Goal, and Who Will Support Me?

The focus of the second phase is on students seeking heroes, role models, and mentors who will act as support systems as they pursue their individual goals from phase one. These individuals should be people who have accomplished goals similar to the ones students have identified. To accomplish this, students typically must conduct research and gather information about individuals who might be heroes, role models, and mentors. This is an excellent opportunity for students to practice the cognitive skill of navigating digital sources (see table 9.1 in chapter 9, pages 112–113) by gathering information from the Internet or library sources. Teachers can make a distinction between mentors and heroes or role models by explaining that mentors are people with whom students can actually interact. Even if mentors have not accomplished the same goals toward which students are striving, they can be a source of encouragement.

Phase Three: What Skills and Resources Will I Need to Accomplish My Goal?

During phase three, students gather information about what is required to accomplish their goals. In contrast to phase one (where the focus is on thinking without fear of failure), phase three is focused on the hard facts regarding the accomplishment of a challenging goal. Students must determine the steps they will need to take to accomplish their goal and what information and skills they will need to implement those steps. Like phase two, this phase is an excellent opportunity for students to practice cognitive skills like generating conclusions.

Phase Four: What Will I Have to Change to Achieve My Goal?

Of all the phases associated with personal projects, this one is the most challenging and confrontational because students must identify how their current behavior needs to change to accomplish their goals. Stated differently, students must confront scripts they have that are getting in their way. Willingness to change a personal behavior (that is, a script) that is not contributing to the achievement of one's goals is the centerpiece of all truly notable accomplishments. Teachers can facilitate this phase if they are willing to share their own scripts that get in the way of accomplishing their goals.

Phase Five: What Is My Plan for Achieving My Goal, and How Hard Will I Have to Work?

During the fifth phase, students write a concrete plan to accomplish their goals. This is a metacognitive function. The plan is a general outline for future actions and decisions, and students should recognize that revisions may need to be made to their plans as various circumstances and opportunities arise. Even so, plans should be as detailed as possible and should include milestones and significant events. Detailed plans help make goals and the actions associated with them clearer and more real in students' minds.

Phase Six: What Small Steps Can I Take Right Now?

Phase six is designed to help students identify things they can do immediately to set themselves on the path toward achieving their goals. These are referred to as short-term goals. Teachers can explain to students that accomplishing short-term goals that only take a few days or weeks can help them accomplish their long-term goals. In fact, accomplishing long-term goals can be defined as accomplishing a series of related short-term goals. As students set short-term goals (or small steps), they should write them down and give them to the teacher. The teacher then returns the goals to the student after the due date for the small step.

Phase Seven: How Have I Been Doing, and What Have I Learned About Myself?

As students set and achieve short-term goals and evaluate whether or not they met those goals, the teacher can ask them to examine how well things are going and identify corrections they need to make in their behavior. Personal projects will eventually end (at least in terms of class time spent on them). When such a time comes, it is useful to ask students to reflect on what they have learned about themselves as a result of their personal project. Teachers should share the same.

The Transformed Classroom

The classroom of the teacher who seeks to both instruct and awaken the learner in some ways will look very similar to most classrooms in the United States. Students will receive instruction in critical content for specific subject areas. Students will also receive instruction in and opportunities for applying cognitive skills. In addition to these fairly common activities, the classroom of the teacher who seeks to both instruct and awaken the learner will involve activities that are relatively rare. Students will be involved in discussions about how human beings operate; they will apply what they have learned about human behavior to examine and gain more control over their own behaviors. Students will also engage in long-term projects that allow them to pursue goals that operationalize deeply held beliefs and dreams. Finally, the classroom of the teacher who seeks to both instruct and awaken the learner will be a place of acceptance and support that continually seeks to inspire students.

CHAPTER 12

The School That Instructs and Awakens the Learner

*Education is that whole system of human
training within and without the school
house walls, which molds and develops men.*

—W. E. B. Du Bois

Just as the classroom designed to instruct and awaken the learner will have things in common with traditional classrooms, the school designed to instruct and awaken the learner will have things in common with traditional schools. Instruction will be provided in critical content, and cognitive skills will be taught and applied to that content. However, even within these relatively common activities, the school will have some marked departures from the norm.

A Clear Progression of Knowledge

In the school designed to instruct and awaken the learner, the critical content on which instruction is provided will be organized to guide students through a progression of knowledge from simple to complex content. Such a structure is frequently referred to as a *learning progression*. Maryann Wiggs (2011) provided a description of a learning progression for the English language arts topic of "Analyze how and why individuals, events, and ideas develop and interact over the course of a text" (NGA & CCSSO, 2010, p. 10). Marzano and colleagues (2013) provided an adaptation of this process, depicted in figure 12.1.

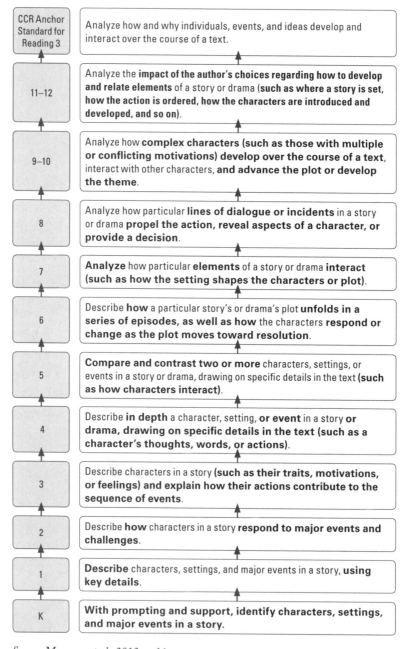

Source: Marzano et al., 2013, p. 16.

Figure 12.1: Learning progression in English language arts.

This progression starts with a rather simple manifestation of the analysis skill and progresses to a rather complex manifestation. At the kindergarten level, students are simply expected to identify characters, settings, and major events in a story when prompted by the teacher. By grades 11 and 12, students are expected to analyze the impact of the author's choices about where the story is set, how action is ordered, and how characters are introduced and developed. Between these two ends of the learning progression, the expectations form scaffolding that gradually takes the student from the simplest to the most complex aspects of this skill.

Learning progressions add a feature to the curriculum that can help students acquire a growth mindset; as we have seen, that is a powerful self-system perspective. Progressions provide students with a clear picture of where they are and what they need to do to get to the next level. As they work through the progression, students observe the relationship between their academic growth and their level of effort. The harder they work, the more they learn. The relationship between effort and progress can be made even more salient if the school systematically reports status and growth.

Reporting Status and Growth

Both status and growth can be compiled and reported on a systematic basis at the individual student level. Figure 12.2 (pages 168–171) depicts how such a report could look for one particular student.

Notice that this report has multiple bars for the subject areas of mathematics, science, and social studies. Each bar in figure 12.2 represents a different topic within a specific subject area. For example, English language arts reports this particular student's status and growth in four broad areas (commonly referred to as *strands*): Reading, Writing, Speaking and Listening, and Language. Each broad area contains bar graphs for very specific topics such as Questioning, Inference, and Interpretation within the strand of Reading.

English Language Arts

Reading	Summative Score	0.0	0.5	1.0	1.5	2.0	2.5	3.0	3.5	4.0
Questioning, Inference, and Interpretation	3.0									
Themes and Central Ideas	2.0									
Argument and Reasoning	2.5									
Writing	**Summative Score**	0.0	0.5	1.0	1.5	2.0	2.5	3.0	3.5	4.0
Argumentative	2.0									
Task, Purpose, and Audience	2.5									
Research	3.5									
Speaking and Listening	**Summative Score**	0.0	0.5	1.0	1.5	2.0	2.5	3.0	3.5	4.0
Speech Writing	2.5									
Presentation and Delivery	2.0									

Language	Summative Score	0.0	0.5	1.0	1.5	2.0	2.5	3.0	3.5	4.0
Grammar	3.0									
Language Conventions	2.0									
Cognitive Skills in Reading	**Summative Score**	0.0	0.5	1.0	1.5	2.0	2.5	3.0	3.5	4.0
Identifying Basic Relationships Between Ideas	3.0									
Generating and Manipulating Mental Images	1.5									
Number and Quantity	**Summative Score**	0.0	0.5	1.0	1.5	2.0	2.5	3.0	3.5	4.0
Fractions	4.0									
Adding and Subtracting Fractions	2.5									

Mathematics

Continued↓

Figure 12.2: Sample student status and growth report.

Operations and Algebra	Summative Score	0.0	0.5	1.0	1.5	2.0	2.5	3.0	3.5	4.0
Multiplication and Division	3.0									
Expressions and Equations	3.5									

Cognitive Skills in Mathematics	Summative Score	0.0	0.5	1.0	1.5	2.0	2.5	3.0	3.5	4.0
Identifying Basic Relationships Between Ideas	3.0									
Generating and Manipulating Mental Images	2.5									

Science

	Summative Score	0.0	0.5	1.0	1.5	2.0	2.5	3.0	3.5	4.0
Earth Materials and Systems	2.5									
Natural Resources	3.0									
Role of Water	2.5									

Cognitive Skills in Science	Summative Score	0.0	0.5	1.0	1.5	2.0	2.5	3.0	3.5	4.0
Identifying Basic Relationships Between Ideas	2.5									
Generating and Manipulating Mental Images	3.0									

Social Studies

	Summative Score	0.0	0.5	1.0	1.5	2.0	2.5	3.0	3.5	4.0
Cultural Relationships	2.5									
Physical Environments and Immigration	2.0									

Cognitive Skills in Social Studies	Summative Score	0.0	0.5	1.0	1.5	2.0	2.5	3.0	3.5	4.0
Identifying Basic Relationships Between Ideas	3.0									
Generating and Manipulating Mental Images	2.5									

It is also important to note that bar graphs report status and growth for the cognitive skills described in chapter 9. For example, in English language arts, status and growth are reported for the cognitive skills of Identifying Basic Relationships Between Ideas, and Generating and Manipulating Mental Images.

The shading in each bar graph provides useful information to support the growth mindset. The dark part of each bar graph represents a student's status at the beginning of the year. The light part represents the student's status at the time when the report is issued. The length of the light part of each bar graph depicts student growth. For example, in figure 12.2, the student has grown from a score of 1.5 to 3.0 for the topic of Questioning, Inference, and Interpretation.

The scale on these bar graphs ranges from 0.0 to 4.0 with half-point intervals. The score of 3.0 is the level that indicates a student is proficient in a particular topic. Each of the bar graphs in figure 12.2 would be accompanied by a proficiency scale like the one in table 12.1.

As shown in table 12.1, three levels of explicit content are articulated in the scale. The target learning goal appears at the 3.0 level of the proficiency scale. A simpler learning goal appears at the 2.0 level, and a more complex learning goal is inserted at the 4.0 level. These levels—2.0, 3.0, and 4.0—are the only ones for which the descriptors change from scale to scale. Descriptors for scores 1.0, 0.0, and all of the half-point scores do not change from one scale to another. Half-point scores indicate that a student has moved beyond one score level but has not yet demonstrated proficiency at the next level. For example, a score of 3.5 indicates competence with all of the content at the 3.0 level and some of the content at the 4.0 level. Similarly, a score of 2.5 indicates competence with all of the content at the 2.0 level but only some of the content at the 3.0 level. A score of 1.5 indicates competence with some of the 2.0 content but none of the content from levels 3.0 or 4.0.

Table 12.1: Proficiency Scale for Interpreting Remainders

Score 4.0	The student will investigate how remainders are expressed (for example, with fractions or decimal notation) or otherwise dealt with (for example, dropping, rounding, or sharing) in the real world.	
	Score 3.5	In addition to score 3.0 performance, partial success at score 4.0 content
Score 3.0	The student will: <ul><li>Solve division word problems in which remainders must be interpreted</li></ul>	
	Score 2.5	No major errors or omissions regarding score 2.0 content, and partial success at score 3.0 content
Score 2.0	The student will recognize or recall specific vocabulary, such as: <ul><li>*Dividend, divisor, remainder*</li></ul> The student will perform basic processes, such as: <ul><li>Identify remainders when solving division number problems (non-word problems)</li></ul>	
	Score 1.5	Partial success at score 2.0 content, and major errors or omissions regarding score 3.0 content
Score 1.0	With help, partial success at score 2.0 content and score 3.0 content	
	Score 0.5	With help, partial success at score 2.0 content but not at score 3.0 content
Score 0.0	Even with help, no success	

Source: Marzano et al., 2013, p. 50.

This system of reporting makes a student's status clear at any given moment in time and helps students identify what they need to do to improve. Using this form of reporting, a student can set specific goals, create a plan for accomplishing those goals, and monitor his or her progress toward their goals—all important metacognitive processes. When challenged by the goals they set, students can examine their reactions and employ what they know about the self-system to cultivate a stronger sense of self-efficacy.

Ultimately, the organization of content into learning progressions (as shown in figure 12.1, page 166) and the status and growth system depicted in figure 12.2 (pages 168–171) will lead a school to consider a competency-based approach.

A Competency-Based Approach

As described by Marzano (2010), in a competency-based system students are not locked into a specific grade level based on their age. Rather, they move up to the next level of content when they have demonstrated mastery at the previous level of content. Therefore, instead of grades, competency-based approaches use content-based levels of knowledge and skill for each subject area. The report card in table 12.2 shows a student's status across a variety of subject areas in a competency-based system.

In table 12.2, not all subject areas have the same number of levels; some have ten, others have seven, six, or five. This is because, in a competency-based system, the number of levels in a content area is determined by the nature of the content in that area. In some areas, such as mathematics, language arts, science, or social studies, the content might logically fall into ten levels. In others, such as art or technology, fewer levels might be more appropriate. For all levels, the highest numbered level indicates the level of mastery required for high school graduation. This convention aligns with a key tenet of competency-based systems: the content is organized into natural progressions (that is, learning progressions) of information and skill rather than artificial grade levels based on age. Also notice in table 12.2 that some subject areas have one or more advanced levels. These levels are designed to allow students to further their learning beyond the high school graduation requirements if they so desire.

In a competency-based system, students are instructed at their current level of mastery in each subject area. For example, the student whose scores are reported in table 12.2 is working at level

Table 12.2: Competency-Based Report Card

Level	Art	Career Literacy	Math	Personal/ Social Skills	Language Arts	Science	Social Studies	Technology
(Advanced) 3								
(Advanced) 2								
(Advanced) 1								
10								
09								
08								
07								
06								
05								
04		2 of 16	21 of 35		3 of 36	17 of 25		
03	9 of 10	3.0 (Proficient)	3.0 (Proficient)	4 of 6	4.0 (Advanced)	3.0 (Proficient)	13 of 15	7 of 8
02	3.0 (Proficient)	3.0 (Proficient)	4.0 (Advanced)	3.0 (Proficient)	3.0 (Proficient)	3.0 (Proficient)	3.0 (Proficient)	4.0 (Advanced)
01	3.0 (Proficient)	3.0 (Proficient)	4.0 (Advanced)	3.0 (Proficient)	3.0 (Proficient)	3.0 (Proficient)	3.0 (Proficient)	4.0 (Advanced)

Note: Shaded cells indicate levels that do not apply to a subject area.

Source: Marzano, 2010, p. 119.

3 for art, personal/social skills, social studies, and technology, and at level 4 for career literacy, math, language arts, and science. To accommodate learning at various levels, depending on the subject area, schools have several options. The most obvious is for students to move to different teachers for each subject. The student would meet with the level 3 teacher for art, the level 4 teacher for mathematics, the level 3 teacher for social studies, and so on. Alternatively, teachers might teach multiple levels. In that case, teacher A would teach mathematics levels 1, 2, and 3, teacher B would teach mathematics levels 4, 5, and 6, and so on. Students would meet with the teacher who taught their current level. For more information on how to address scheduling, logistics, and staffing in a competency-based system, see *Delivering on the Promise* (DeLorenzo, Battino, Schreiber, & Gaddy Carrio, 2009).

Finally, notice that in table 12.2, the student's current status is reported for each subject area. For example, in mathematics, the student is working on level 4 and has a ratio of "21 of 35" recorded. This indicates that the student has demonstrated competence (score 3.0 or higher) on twenty-one of the thirty-five learning goals at level 4. To move to level 5 in mathematics, this student must demonstrate competence on fourteen more learning goals. In art, the student is at level 3 and has a ratio of "9 of 10." Therefore, the student must demonstrate competence with one more learning goal to move to level 4 in art. In competency-based systems, no overall grades are computed. Instead, the emphasis is on demonstrating proficiency in every learning goal associated with a level before progressing to the next level.

As stated previously, competency-based systems do not employ traditional grade levels. For some schools and districts, however, this shift represents too radical of a change from the norm. That is, some schools and districts want to use a competency-based approach while maintaining traditional grade levels. Fortunately, this is possible. The most straightforward way to accomplish this is to simply treat grade levels as performance levels. This type of record-keeping system up to eighth grade is depicted in table 12.3 (page 178).

Notice that table 12.3 is almost identical to table 12.2 except that the performance levels have been replaced by grade levels. Each grade level has a specific number of learning goals associated with it, and students move through the grade levels by demonstrating competency (score 3.0 or higher) on all of the learning goals for a grade level.

Competency-based report cards at the high school level might list specific courses for each subject area, in order from simpler courses to more complex courses. For example, in mathematics, Algebra I would be listed before Algebra II because it addresses simpler content. Table 12.4 (page 179) depicts such a report card at the high school level.

In some cases, certain courses will not fall into a strict hierarchy. For example, in technology, Desktop Publishing does not necessarily have to be taken before Digital Graphics and Animation. As with the performance or grade levels in tables 12.2 or 12.3, students must demonstrate mastery (score 3.0 or higher) for all of the learning goals associated with a specific course before they receive credit for that course.

When using traditional grade levels with competency-based grading, overall omnibus grades are not assigned to students. Rather, as shown in tables 12.3 and 12.4, a ratio is recorded for the grade level the student is working on in each subject area. The ratio represents the number of learning goals for which the student has demonstrated mastery (score 3.0 or higher).

As shown in tables 12.2, 12.3, and 12.4, the lowest score that a student can receive for any level, grade level, or course is 3.0 (Proficient). This is because students must demonstrate mastery at the score 3.0 level or higher on each learning goal in a level, grade level, or course to move on to the next level, grade level, or course. However, distinctions can still be made between students'

Table 12.3: Competency-Based Reporting for Grades K–8

Grade	Art	Career Literacy	Math	Personal/ Social Skills	Language Arts	Science	Social Studies	Technology
8								
7								
6								
5			4 of 32					
4		7 of 11	3.0 (Proficient)		7 of 31	2 of 23		
3		3.0 (Proficient)	4.0 (Advanced)	2 of 6	3.0 (Proficient)	4.0 (Advanced)		
2	9 of 10	3.0 (Proficient)	3.0 (Proficient)	3.0 (Proficient)	4.0 (Advanced)	3.0 (Proficient)	2 of 15	7 of 8
1	3.0 (Proficient)	3.0 (Proficient)	4.0 (Advanced)	3.0 (Proficient)	3.0 (Proficient)	3.0 (Proficient)	3.0 (Proficient)	4.0 (Advanced)
K	3.0 (Proficient)	3.0 (Proficient)	4.0 (Advanced)	3.0 (Proficient)	3.0 (Proficient)	3.0 (Proficient)	3.0 (Proficient)	3.0 (Proficient)

Source: Marzano, 2010, p. 121.

Table 12.4: Competency-Based Reporting for High School

Subject Area	Course	Score
Mathematics	Calculus	
	Geometry	
	Algebra II	12 of 24
	Algebra I	3.0 (Proficient)
Science	AP Environmental Science	
	Physics	
	Chemistry	6 of 22
	Biology	3.0 (Proficient)
Social Studies	Economics	
	World History	11 of 21
	U.S. History	4.0 (Advanced)
	Geography	3.0 (Proficient)
Language Arts	Shakespeare	
	Ancient Literature	13 of 22
	European Literature	3.0 (Proficient)
	U.S. Literature	3.0 (Proficient)
Art	Orchestra	
	Performing Arts	9 of 21
	Painting	3.0 (Proficient)
Technology	Digital Graphics and Animation	
	Desktop Publishing	17 of 22
	Computer Science	4.0 (Advanced)

Source: Marzano, 2010, p. 121.

performances within each level, grade level, or course. Notice that in table 12.2 (page 175), the row for level 1 indicates that the student achieved scores of 4.0 (Advanced) in mathematics and technology and scores of 3.0 (Proficient) in all other subjects. Recall that students must demonstrate mastery on each learning goal by achieving score 3.0 *or higher*. If a student achieves a score of 4.0 on all (or a majority) of the learning goals for a particular level of a subject area, he or she can be awarded the final status of 4.0 (Advanced) for that level in the subject area.

As with schools that use performance levels, schools that implement competency-based grading using grade levels will need to consider scheduling. Grade-level bands are one way to address scheduling within a grade-level competency-based approach. For example, a school might be organized as shown in table 12.5.

Table 12.5: Grade-Level Bands

High School (9–12)
Remedial
Advanced
6–8
Remedial
Advanced
3–5
Remedial
Advanced
K–2
Remedial

Source: Marzano, 2010, p. 122.

Table 12.5 depicts four grade-level bands: K–2, 3–5, 6–8, and hight school (9–12). Within each band, classes for a particular subject area are offered at the same time. For example, within the 3–5 band, all mathematics classes (for grades 3, 4, and 5) are offered at the same time, all science classes (for grades 3, 4, and 5) are offered at the same time, and so forth. Additionally, advanced and remedial classes for each subject area are offered concurrently with the grade-level band classes. These classes are for students working above and below the grade-level interval (in this case, 3–5). The advanced classes allow students to progress as rapidly as they wish through mathematics content at grade 6 and higher. The focus of the remedial classes is to bring students working below the third-grade level up to that level as quickly as possible.

One advantage of the grade-level approach to a competency-based system is that students' cohort groups are preserved. For example, students might have a homeroom period and activities that are specific to their grade level. High schools could still maintain freshman, sophomore, junior, and senior classes. The concept of grade-level cohorts is deeply engrained in American culture and society. Therefore, an approach to competency-based schooling that preserves grade-level cohorts while still allowing students to work on the content appropriate to their current levels of understanding and skill in each subject is very useful.

The Transformed School

The school that employs a competency-based approach is in a position to transform the experience of K–12 education for all students. As in a traditional school, the students in a competency-based school will receive instruction in important content and analyze that content through judicious use of the cognitive skills. However, this is currently available in some high-functioning traditional schools. In competency-based systems, students have the additional advantage of moving through knowledge levels at their own pace. Consequently, there are no intervals of time when students are forced to work on content they already know. Additionally, there are no intervals of time when students are forced to learn content for which they have not been adequately prepared. This free-flowing and self-paced movement simultaneously provides challenges to each student and recognition of goals that have been accomplished. The competency-based system is by definition a mechanism that can both instruct and awaken the learner. These dual purposes are not as easily accomplished in the traditional system.

Epilogue

In one sense, this book has described a possible future for K–12 education, one in which students are prepared not only to participate in the world of the 21st century but also to change the world of the 21st century for the better. Perhaps the success or failure of that world is dependent, at least in part, on the education system through which students matriculate.

In another sense, this book has been a "call to arms" for educators. The possible future of education articulated in the previous chapters will occur only if educators in the present system are inspired and then act on their inspiration. In Bob's words, educators must examine their basic operating principles and find those that compel them to take actions that might have lain dormant for decades. In Darrell's words, educators must see through the current system to a philosophy that holds the heart, head, and hands in harmony and create systems that impart transformation rather than simply communicating information.

Hopefully this book has provided both a vision as to what the future of education can be and the inspiration to manifest that vision!

References and Resources

Amen, D. G. (1998). *Change your brain, change your life: The breakthrough program for conquering anxiety, depression, obsessiveness, anger, and impulsiveness.* New York: Times Books.

Anderson, J. R. (1983). *The architecture of cognition.* Cambridge, MA: Harvard University Press.

Argyris, C., & Schön, D. (1974). *Theory in practice: Increasing professional effectiveness.* San Francisco: Jossey-Bass.

Argyris, C., & Schön, D. (1978). *Organizational learning: A theory of action perspective.* Reading, MA: Addison-Wesley.

B'Hahn, C. (2001). Be the change you wish to see: An interview with Arun Gandhi. *Reclaiming Children and Youth, 10*(1), 6–9.

Binns, K., & Markow, D. (1999). *The Metropolitan Life survey of the American teacher, 1999: Violence in America's public schools—Five years later.* New York: Harris.

Blake, W. (1917). The everlasting gospel. In D. H. S. Nicholson & A. H. E. Lee (Eds.), *The Oxford book of English mystical verse* (pp. 94–103). Oxford, England: The Clarendon Press.

Brown, A. L. (1978). Knowing when, where and how to remember: A problem of metacognition. In R. Glaser (Ed.), *Advances in instructional psychology* (Vol. 1, pp. 77–165). Hillsdale, NJ: Erlbaum.

Brown, A. L. (1980). Metacognitive development and reading. In R. J. Spiro, B. C. Bruce, & W. F. Brewer (Eds.), *Theoretical issues in reading comprehension: Perspectives from cognitive psychology, linguistics, artificial intelligence, and education* (pp. 453–481). Hillsdale, NJ: Erlbaum.

Brown, A. L. (1984). Metacognition, executive control, self-regulation, and other even more mysterious mechanisms. In F. E. Weinert & R. H. Kluwe (Eds.), *Metacognition, motivation, and learning* (pp. 60–108). Stuttgart, West Germany: Kuhlhammer.

Brühlmeier, A., & Kuhlemann, G. (2013). *Stans and the letter from Stans.* Accessed at www.heinrich-pestalozzi.de/en /documentation/biography/stans/index.htm on January 28, 2014.

Burgoon, J. K., Guerrero, L. K., & Floyd, K. (2009). *Nonverbal communication.* New York: Allyn & Bacon.

Burnett, F. H. (1987). *The secret garden.* New York: Signet Classics. (Original work published 1911)

Campbell, J. (2004). *Pathways to bliss: Mythology and personal transformation.* Novato, CA: New World Library.

Colegrove, C. P. (1910). *The teacher and the school.* New York: Scribner's Sons.

Compayré, G. (1893). *Psychology applied to education.* Boston: Heath.

Covey, S. R. (2004). *The 7 habits of highly effective people: Powerful lessons in personal change.* New York: Free Press.

Cross, S. E., & Markus, H. R. (1994). Self-schemas, possible selves, and competent performance. *Journal of Educational Psychology, 86*(3), 423–438.

Csikszentmihalyi, M. (1990). *Flow: The psychology of optimal experience.* New York: Harper & Row.

Deci, E. L. (1995). *Why we do what we do: The dynamics of personal autonomy.* New York: Putnam's Sons.

Deci, E. L., Connell, J. P., & Ryan, R. M. (1989). Self-determination in a work organization. *Journal of Applied Psychology, 74*(4), 580–590.

Deci, E. L., Koestner, R., & Ryan, R. M. (1999). A meta-analytic review of experiments examining the effects of extrinsic rewards on intrinsic motivation. *Psychological Bulletin, 125*(6), 627–668.

Deci, E. L., & Ryan, R. M. (1987). The support of autonomy and the control of behavior. *Journal of Personality and Social Psychology, 53*(6), 1024–1037.

Deci, E. L., & Ryan, R. M. (2008a). A self-determination theory approach to psychotherapy: The motivational basis for effective change. *Canadian Psychology, 49*(3), 186–193.

Deci, E. L., & Ryan, R. M. (2008b). Self-determination theory: A macrotheory of human motivation, development, and health. *Canadian Psychology, 49*(3), 182–185.

de Guimps, R. (1889). *Pestalozzi: His aim and work.* Syracuse, NY: Bardeen.

DeLorenzo, R. A., Battino, W. J., Schreiber, R. M., & Gaddy Carrio, B. G. (2009). *Delivering on the promise: The education revolution.* Bloomington, IN: Solution Tree Press.

DeVito, D. (Producer), Shamberg, M. (Producer), Sher, S. (Producer), & LaGravenese, R. (Director). (2007). *Freedom writers* [Motion picture]. United States: Paramount Pictures.

Diener, C. I., & Dweck, C. S. (1978). An analysis of learned helplessness: Continuous changes in performance, strategy, and achievement cognitions following failure. *Journal of Personality and Social Psychology, 36*(5), 451–462.

Diller, D. (2008). *Spaces & places: Designing classrooms for literacy.* Portland, ME: Stenhouse.

Dweck, C. S. (2000). *Self-theories: Their role in motivation, personality, and development.* New York: Psychology Press.

Dweck, C. S. (2006). *Mindset: The new psychology of success.* New York: Random House.

Dweck, C. S., & Master, A. (2009). Self-theories and motivation: Students' beliefs about intelligence. In K. R. Wentzel & A. Wigfield (Eds.), *Handbook of motivation at school* (pp. 123–140). New York: Routledge.

Einstein, A. (2009). *Einstein on cosmic religion: And other opinions and aphorisms.* Mineola, NY: Dover. (Original work published 1931)

Flavell, J. H. (1978). Metacognitive development. In J. M. Scandura & C. J. Brainerd (Eds.), *Structural-process theories of complex human behavior: Proceedings of the NATO Advanced Study Institute on Structural/Process Theories of Complex Human Behavior, Banff, Alberta, Canada, June 18–26, 1977* (pp. 213–245). Alphen aan den Rijn, Netherlands: Sijthoff and Noordhoff.

Flavell, J. H. (1979). Metacognition and cognitive monitoring: A new area of cognitive-developmental inquiry. *American Psychologist, 34*(10), 906–911.

Flavell, J. H. (1987). Speculations about the nature and development of metacognition. In F. E. Weinert & R. H. Kluwe (Eds.), *Metacognition, motivation and understanding* (pp. 21–29). Hillsdale, NJ: Erlbaum.

Frederiksen, N. (1984). Implications of cognitive theory for instruction in problem solving. *Review of Educational Research, 54*(3), 363–387.

Fried, S., & Fried, P. (1996). *Bullies and victims: Helping your child survive the schoolyard battlefield.* New York: Evans.

Froebel, F. (1908). *The education of man.* New York: Appleton.

Gaddy, B. B., Hall, T. W., & Marzano, R. J. (1996). *School wars: Resolving our conflicts over religion and values.* San Francisco: Jossey-Bass.

Gilovich, T. (1991). *How we know what isn't so: The fallibility of human reason in everyday life.* New York: Free Press.

Goleman, D. (1995). *Emotional intelligence: Why it can matter more than IQ.* New York: Bantam Books.

Gonzalez, J. (2010, May 25). High-school dropout rate is cited as a key barrier to Obama's college-completion goal. *The Chronicle of Higher Education.* Accessed at http://chronicle.com/article/High-School-Dropout-Rate-%20%20%20%20Is/65669 on January 2, 2014.

Goodenow, C. (1993). Classroom belonging among early adolescent students: Relationships to motivation and achievement. *Journal of Early Adolescence, 13*(1), 21–43.

Grant, A. M. (2013). *Give and take: A revolutionary approach to success.* New York: Viking.

Hoose, P. M. (1993). *It's our world, too! Stories of young people who are making a difference.* Boston: Joy Street Books.

Hoyt, C. O. (1908). *Studies in the history of modern education.* New York: Silver, Burdett.

Hume, D. (1898). *A treatise of human nature: Being an attempt to introduce the experimental method of reasoning into moral subjects.* London: Longmans, Green.

Humphrey, S. M. (2005). *Dare to dream! 25 extraordinary lives.* Amherst, NY: Prometheus Books.

Jacobs, J. (1914). *Æsops's fables* (Vol. XVII, Part 1). New York: P.F. Collier & Son. Accessed at www.bartleby.com/17/1/72.html on April 7, 2014.

Kain, E. (2011, March 8). *High teacher turnover rates are a big problem for America's public schools.* Accessed at www.forbes.com/sites/erikkain/2011/03/08/high-teacher-turnover-rates-are-a-big-problem-for-americas-public-schools on January 2, 2014.

Kendall, J. S., & Marzano, R. J. (2000). *Content knowledge: A compendium of standards and benchmarks for K–12 education* (3rd ed.). Alexandria, VA: Association for Supervision and Curriculum Development.

Knapp, M. L., & Hall, J. A. (2010). *Nonverbal communication in human interaction* (7th ed.). Boston: Wadsworth Cengage Learning.

Kotulak, R. (1996). *Inside the brain: Revolutionary discoveries of how the mind works.* Kansas City, MO: Andrews and McMeel.

Ladd, G. W., Herald-Brown, S. L., & Kochel, K. P. (2009). Peers and motivation. In K. R. Wentzel & A. Wigfield (Eds.), *Handbook of motivation at school* (pp. 323–348). New York: Routledge.

Langer, E. J. (1989). *Mindfulness*. Reading, MA: Addison-Wesley.

Langer, E. J., & Rodin, J. (1976). The effects of enhanced personal responsibility for the aged: A field experiment in an institutional setting. *Journal of Personality and Social Psychology, 34*(2), 191–198.

Langer, E. J., & Weinman, C. (1981). When thinking disrupts intellectual performance: Mindlessness on an overlearned task. *Personality and Social Psychology Bulletin, 7*(2), 240–243.

Lewis, B. A. (1992). *Kids with courage: True stories about young people making a difference*. Minneapolis, MN: Free Spirit.

Los Angeles Police Department. (2014). *Why young people join gangs*. Accessed at www.lapdonline.org/top_ten_most_wanted_gang_members/content_basic_view/23473 on January 6, 2014.

Markus, H., & Nurius, P. (1986). Possible selves. *American Psychologist, 41*(9), 954–969.

Markus, H., & Ruvolo, A. (1989). Possible selves: Personalized representations of goals. In L. A. Pervin (Ed.), *Goal concepts in personality and social psychology* (pp. 211–241). Hillsdale, NJ: Erlbaum.

Marzano, R. J. (1998). Cognitive, metacognitive, and conative considerations in classroom assessment. In N. M. Lambert & B. L. McCombs (Eds.), *How students learn: Reforming schools through learner-centered education* (pp. 241–266). Washington, DC: American Psychological Association.

Marzano, R. J. (with Marzano, J. S., & Pickering, D. J.). (2003a). *Classroom management that works: Research-based strategies for every teacher*. Alexandria, VA: Association for Supervision and Curriculum Development.

Marzano, R. J. (2003b). *What works in schools: Translating research into action.* Alexandria, VA: Association for Supervision and Curriculum Development.

Marzano, R. J. (2006). *Classroom assessment and grading that work.* Alexandria, VA: Association for Supervision and Curriculum Development.

Marzano, R. J. (2007). *The art and science of teaching: A comprehensive framework for effective instruction.* Alexandria, VA: Association for Supervision and Curriculum Development.

Marzano, R. J. (2010). *Formative assessment and standards-based grading.* Bloomington, IN: Marzano Research.

Marzano, R. J., Brandt, R. S., Hughes, C. S., Jones, B. F., Presseisen, B. Z., Rankin, S. C., et al. (1988). *Dimensions of thinking: A framework for curriculum and instruction.* Alexandria, VA: Association for Supervision and Curriculum Development.

Marzano, R. J., & Haystead, M. W. (2008). *Making standards useful in the classroom.* Alexandria, VA: Association for Supervision and Curriculum Development.

Marzano, R. J., & Heflebower, T. (2012). *Teaching & assessing 21st century skills.* Bloomington, IN: Marzano Research.

Marzano, R. J., & Kendall, J. S. (with Gaddy, B. B.). (1999). *Essential knowledge: The debate over what American students should know.* Aurora, CO: Mid-continent Research for Education and Learning.

Marzano, R. J., & Kendall, J. S. (2007). *The new taxonomy of educational objectives* (2nd ed.). Thousand Oaks, CA: Corwin Press.

Marzano, R. J., & Marzano, J. (1988). Toward a cognitive theory of commitment and its implications for therapy. *Psychotherapy in Private Practice, 6*(4), 69–81.

Marzano, R. J., & Marzano, J. (2010). The inner game of teaching. In R. Marzano (Ed.), *On excellence in teaching* (pp. 345–367). Bloomington, IN: Solution Tree Press.

Marzano, R. J., Paynter, D. E., & Doty, J. K. (2003). *The pathfinder project: Exploring the power of one—Teacher's manual.* Conifer, CO: Pathfinder Education.

Marzano, R. J., & Pickering, D. J. (with Arredondo, D. E., Blackburn, G. J., Brandt, R. S., Moffett, C. A., Paynter, D. E., Pollock, J. E., & Whisler, J. S.). (1997). *Dimensions of learning: Teacher's manual* (2nd ed.). Alexandria, VA: Association for Supervision and Curriculum Development.

Marzano, R. J., & Pickering, D. J. (with Heflebower, T.). (2011). *The highly engaged classroom.* Bloomington, IN: Marzano Research.

Marzano, R. J., Yanoski, D. C., Hoegh, J. K., & Simms, J. A. (with Heflebower, T., & Warrick, P.). (2013). *Using Common Core standards to enhance classroom instruction & assessment.* Bloomington, IN: Marzano Research.

Matsumoto, D., Frank, M. G., & Hwang, H. S. (Eds.). (2013). *Nonverbal communication: Science and applications.* Thousand Oaks, CA: SAGE.

McCombs, B. L. (1984). Processes and skills underlying intrinsic motivation to learn: Toward a definition of motivational skills training intervention. *Educational Psychologist, 19*(4), 197–218.

McCombs, B. L. (1986). The role of the self-system in self-regulated learning. *Contemporary Educational Psychology, 11*(4), 314–332.

McCombs, B. L. (1989). Self-regulated learning and academic achievement: A phenomenological view. In B. J. Zimmerman & D. H. Schunk (Eds.), *Self-regulated learning and academic achievement: Theory, research and practice* (pp. 51–82). New York: Springer-Verlag.

McCombs, B., & Marzano, R. J. (1990). Putting the self in self-regulated learning: The self as agent in integrating will and skill. *Educational Psychologist, 25*(1), 51–69.

Mehrabian, A. (1972). *Nonverbal communication.* New York: Aldine.

Meichenbaum, D., & Asarnow, J. (1979). Cognitive-behavioral modification and metacognitive development: Implications for the classroom. In P. C. Kendall & S. D. Hollon (Eds.), *Cognitive-behavioral interventions: Theory, research, and procedures* (pp. 11–35). New York: Academic.

Mervis, C. B. (1980). Category structure and the development of categorization. In R. J. Spiro, B. C. Bruce, & W. F. Brewer (Eds.), *Theoretical issues in reading comprehension: Perspectives from cognitive psychology, linguistics, artificial intelligence, and education* (pp. 279–307). Hillsdale, NJ: Erlbaum.

metamorphosis. (n.d.). *The American heritage new dictionary of cultural literacy* (3rd ed.). Accessed at http://dictionary.reference.com/browse/metamorphosis on March 24, 2014.

National Governors Association Center for Best Practices & Council of Chief State School Officers. (2010). *Common Core State Standards for English language arts & literacy in history/social studies, science, and technical subjects.* Washington, DC: Authors.

Navarro, J. (with Karlins, M.). (2008). *What every BODY is saying: An ex-FBI agent's guide to speed reading people.* New York: HarperCollins.

Northend, C. (1859). *The teacher's assistant: Or hints and methods in school discipline and instruction; Being a series of familiar letters to one entering upon the teacher's work.* Boston: Crosby, Nichols, Lee.

Pease, B., & Pease, A. (2004). *The definitive book of body language.* New York: Bantam Books.

Pekrun, R. (2009, December 23). *Student emotions.* Accessed at www.education.com/reference/article/student-emotions on January 30, 2014.

Pert, C. (1997). *Molecules of emotion: Why you feel the way you feel.* New York: Touchstone.

Raub, A. N. (1883). *Methods of teaching: Including the nature, object, and laws of education, methods of instruction, and methods of culture.* Philadelphia: Fireside.

Rich, M. (2012, December 11). U.S. students still lag globally in math and science, tests show. *The New York Times,* p. A15. Accessed at www.nytimes.com/2012/12/11 /education/us-students-still-lag-globally-in-math-and -science-tests-show.html?_r=2& on January 2, 2014.

Rosenthal, R., & Jacobson, L. (1992). *Pygmalion in the classroom: Teacher expectation and pupils' intellectual development* (Expanded ed.). New York: Irvington.

Rothman, R. (2011). *Something in common: The Common Core standards and the next chapter in American education.* Cambridge, MA: Harvard Education Press.

Rowe, H. A. H. (1985). *Problem solving and intelligence.* Hillsdale, NJ: Erlbaum.

Rowe, M. B. (1974). Relation of wait-time and rewards to the development of language, logic and fate control: Part II—Rewards. *Journal of Research in Science and Teaching, 11*(4), 291–308.

Russell, B. (1967). *Last essay: "1967."* Accessed at http://russell.mcmaster.ca/bressay.htm on April 8, 2014.

Ryan, R. M., & Deci, E. L. (2000). Self-determination theory and the facilitation of intrinsic motivation, social development, and well-being. *American Psychologist, 55*(1), 68–78.

Schank, R. C., & Abelson, R. (1977). *Scripts, plans, goals, and understanding: An inquiry into human knowledge structures.* Hillsdale, NJ: Erlbaum.

Schunk, D. H., & Pajares, F. (2009). Self-efficacy theory. In K. R. Wentzel & A. Wigfield (Eds.), *Handbook of motivation at school* (pp. 35–54). New York: Routledge.

Scott, D. (2013). *Timeless tales to live by.* Littleton, CO: Rachel's Challenge.

Scott, R. (n.d.). *My ethics, my codes of life.* Unpublished essay.

Seligman, M. E. P. (1993). *What you can change and what you can't: The complete guide to successful self-improvement.* New York: Knopf.

Seligman, M. E. P. (2006). *Learned optimism: How to change your mind and your life.* New York: Vintage Books.

Snow, R. E., & Jackson, D. N. (1993). *Assessment of conative constructs for educational research and evaluation: A catalogue* (CSE Tech. Rep. No. 354). Los Angeles: National Center for Research on Evaluation, Standards, and Student Testing. Accessed at www.cse.ucla.edu /products/Reports/TECH354.pdf on March 24, 2014.

Sparks, J. (1844). *The life of Benjamin Franklin: Containing the autobiography with notes and a continuation.* Boston: Tappan and Dennet.

Spiro, R. J., Vispoel, W. L., Schmitz, J. G., Samarapungavan, A., & Boerger, A. E. (1987). Knowledge acquisition for application: Cognitive flexibility and transfer in complex content domains. In B. K. Britton & S. M. Glynn (Eds.), *Executive control processes in reading* (pp. 177–199). Hillsdale, NJ: Erlbaum.

Sternberg, R. J. (1984). Mechanisms of cognitive development: A componential approach. In R. J. Sternberg (Ed.), *Mechanisms of cognitive development* (pp. 163–186). New York: Freeman.

Sternberg, R. J. (1985). *Beyond IQ: A triarchic theory of human intelligence.* New York: Cambridge University Press.

Sternberg, R. J. (1986a). Inside intelligence: Cognitive science enables us to go beyond intelligence tests and understand how the human mind solves problem. *American Scientist, 74*(2), 137–143.

Sternberg, R. J. (1986b). *Intelligence applied: Understanding and increasing your intellectual skills.* New York: Harcourt Brace Jovanovich.

Sticht, T. G., Hofstetter, C. R., & Hofstetter, C. H. (1997). *Knowledge, literacy, and power.* San Diego, CA: Consortium for Workforce Education & Lifelong Learning (CWELL). Accessed at http://scholar.google .com/scholar_url?hl=en&q=http://www.researchgate .net/publication/238711398_Knowledge_Literacy _and_Power/file/e0b4952b2363ed6e22.pdf&sa=X& scisig=AAGBfm019QDoDL14OEyy14amRK9AN wo2Vw&oi=scholarr on April 8, 2014.

Sylwester, R. (2000). *A biological brain in a cultural classroom: Applying biological research to classroom management.* Thousand Oaks, CA: Corwin Press.

University of Salford. (2011). *Improved learning through classroom design.* Accessed at www.salford.ac.uk /business/consultancy/case-studies-nightingale-schools on January 29, 2014.

van Dijk, T. A. (1980). *Macrostructures: An interdisciplinary study of global structures in discourse, interaction, and cognition.* Hillsdale, NJ: Erlbaum.

van Dijk, T. A., & Kintsch, W. (1983). *Strategies of discourse comprehension.* Hillsdale, NJ: Erlbaum.

Violence at schools. (n.d.). Accessed at www.justice.gov/usao /eousa/foia_reading_room/usam/title9/crm00115.htm on January 29, 2014.

Webster, N. (1857). *The elementary spelling book: Being an improvement on "The American Spelling Book."* New York: D. Appleton and Co.

Wentzel, K. R. (2009). Students' relationships with teachers as motivational contexts. In K. R. Wentzel & A. Wigfield (Eds.), *Handbook of motivation at school* (pp. 301–322). New York: Routledge.

White, E. E. (1890). *First book of arithmetic for pupils: Uniting oral and written exercises*. New York: American Book.

White, E. E. (1901). *The art of teaching: A manual for teachers, superintendents, teachers' reading circles, normal schools, training classes, and other persons interested in the right training of the young*. New York: American Book.

Whittier, J. G. (1912). Maud Muller. In T. R. Lounsbury (Ed.), *Yale book of American verse* (pp. 148–152). New Haven, CT: Yale University Press.

Wickelgren, W. A. (1974). *How to solve problems: Elements of a theory of problems and problem solving*. San Francisco: Walt Freeman.

Wiggs, M. D. (2011). Gaining a deeper understanding of the Common Core State Standards: The big picture. In *Navigating implementation of the Common Core State Standards: Getting ready for the Common Core handbook series* (pp. 23–58). Englewood, CO: Lead and Learn Press.

Wise, J. (2009, December 28). When fear makes us superhuman. *Scientific American*. Accessed at www.scientificamerican .com/article.cfm?id=extreme-fear-superhuman on January 6, 2014.

Index

Create a culture of
kindness and compassion

Awaken learners
in your classroom

 Signature PD Service ───────────────────

Awaken the Learner Workshop

Learning Outcomes

- Learn the history and philosophy behind a unique approach to reaching students' hearts.
- Discover ways to create a culture and climate in your classroom that will awaken students to new possibilities.
- Explore a model of behavior, decision making, and engagement that illuminates student motivation and actions in the classroom.
- Consider strategies for effectively and efficiently instructing learners.
- Reflect on your own teaching practices and the extent to which they instill purpose and inspiration in students.

Robert J. Marzano and Darrell Scott

Learn more!

marzanoresearch.com/AwakenWorkshop
888.849.0851